George du Maurier: The Satirist of the Victorians

T. Martin Wood

GEORGE DU MAURIER

THE SATIRIST OF THE VICTORIANS

A REVIEW OF HIS ART AND PERSONALITY

BY T. MARTIN WOOD

WITH FORTY-ONE ILLUSTRATIONS

1913

GEORGE DU MAURIER
FROM A PORTRAIT IN WATER-COLOUR BY HIMSELF.
IN THE POSSESSION OF THE ARTIST'S WIDOW.

PREFACE

Du Maurier worked for periodicals which buried in a back number each phase of his work as it came to an end. Thus it is that he is, unfortunately, chiefly now remembered by the last—the most accessible, but not by any means the finest—period of his work.

The present book is an attempt to correct this and to bring forward du Maurier's name again in the light of his earlier achievement.

No book on the artist, however, would be complete which omitted all reference to his literary attainment; nor would it be in order in an essay of this extent not to seek to demonstrate that connection which always exists between the life and the work of an artist of distinctive temperament. The author has endeavoured, in the chapter devoted to outlining the main incidents of du Maurier's career, to regard the feeling of his representatives that the autobiography of the novels is itself so complete and sensitive as scarcely to call at present for anything supplemental. He wishes to acknowledge the kindness of the artist's family in lending him portraits, sketch-books, and manuscript with the permission for reproduction; also of Mr. W. Lawrence Bradbury, so zealous a guardian of all that redounds to the fame of his great journal, for every kind of assistance; and of Sir Francis Burnand, du Maurier's Editor and comrade, for letters assisting him to form an impression of du Maurier in the flesh. Messrs. Smith, Elder & Co. have also been generous in allowing the reproduction of the four drawings included here, which appeared originally in the *Cornhill Magazine*. The author only wishes that he felt that what he has written more justified this consideration from everyone who was approached in connection with his undertaking.

CONTENTS

ILLUSTRATIONS

There are also several Tailpieces, chronologically arranged

I

THE WORLD OF DU MAURIER

§1

We have in the portfolio of du Maurier the epic of the drawing-room. Many of the Victorians, including the Queen, and Alfred Lord Tennyson, seem to have viewed life from the drawing-room window. They gazed straight across the room from the English hearthrug as from undoubtedly the greatest place on earth. They were probably right. But some of this confidence has gone. Actually in these days there are people who won't own up to having a drawing-room at all. If they have a room that could possibly answer to such a description, they go out of their way to call it the library, though its only available printed matter is a Bradshaw; or the music-room, though the only music ever heard in it is when the piano is dusted.

In turning over the old volumes of *Punch* it is surprising how many of the points made by du Maurier in his drawings and in the legends beneath them still hold good. As a mere "joker" he was perhaps the least able of the *Punch* staff. His influence began when he started inventing imaginary conversations. In many cases these do not represent the discussion of topical subjects at all, but deal with social aberrations, dated only in the illustration by the costume of the time.

In these imaginary conversations he is already a novelist. They record the strokes of finesse and the subterfuges necessary to the attainment of the vain ambitions which are the preoccupation of human genius in superficial levels of Society in all ages. We realise the waste of energy and diplomacy expended to score small points in the social game. His art is a mirror to weed-like qualities of human nature which enjoy a spring-time with every generation. But it also provides a remarkable record of the effect of the sudden replacement of old by new ideals in the world which it depicted.

The rise of the merchant capitalist upon the results of industrial enterprises rendered possible through the invention and rapid perfecting of machinery, created a class who suddenly appeared in the drawing-rooms of the aristocrats as strangers. Du Maurier himself seems to join in the amazement at their intrusion. Much of this first surprise is the theme of his art. Before the death of the artist the newcomers had proved their right to be there, having shamed an Aristocracy, which had lost nearly all its natural occupations, by bringing home to it the fact that the day was over for despising men who traded instead of fighting, who achieved through barter what the brave would once have been too proud to take except by conquest. The business of the original division of human possessions by the sanguinary method was well over; it was now the merchant's day. It was plain that trade could no longer be despised, when, literally in an age of peace and inventive commerce, indolence was the only alternative to engagement in it.

Du Maurier was very tolerant to social intruders when they were pretty. He rather entered into Mrs. de Tomkyns' aims, and showed it by making her pretty. Her ends might not be the highest, but the tact and the subtlety displayed in her campaign were aristocratic in character, and he would not have her laughed at personally, though we may laugh at the topsy-turvy of a Society in which the entrance into a certain drawing-room becomes the fun reward for the perseverance of a lifetime. But du Maurier shuddered when behind this lady, distinguished in the fact of the possession of genius, he saw a multitude of the aspirateless at the door. We never lose upon the face, which showed as his through his art, the expression of well-bred resentment, yet certainly of amusement also.

During the period of du Maurier's work for *Punch* the actor gets his position in Society; and we see desolate gentlemen in other professions drifting about at the back of the room like ships that drag their anchor, while all the feminine blandishment of the place is concentrated on the actor. By following up his drawings we can see the whole surface of Victorian Society change in character; we can see one outrageous innovation after another solidify into what was correct.

There never was a period like the Victorian; in many respects the precedents of all older periods of Society fail to apply. In it the aristocrats believed in democracy, and resented the democrat who was practically their own creation. While the democrat held no faith with the same fervour as his belief that "whatsoever is lovely and of good report" could only be obtained by mingling with the upper classes. It was the commercial glory of the great Industrial Reign that turned the whole character of London Society upside down in du Maurier's time. It became the study of the Suburbs to model themselves on Mayfair, to imitate its "rages" and "crazes" in every shade. It is all the vanities of this emulation which du Maurier records; there is little in his art to betray the great influences Ecclesiastically, scientifically, and politically, which expressed the genius of the Victorians. His splendid Bishops are as tranquil as if the controversial Newman, and Gladstone with his Disestablishment programme, had never disturbed the air. And one fancies that politics must have bored him, so studiously does he through over thirty years avoid even a slanting glance at the events which preoccupied Mr. Punch in his cartoons. There is evidence that there was more than the policy of the Paper in this. Du Maurier was an optimist. An optimist is a man who thinks that everything is going right when it is going wrong. It requires an effort of the imagination to recall and picture the fact that in the first hour of Du Maurier's mere amusement Ruskin was adding his lachrymation to Carlyle's over a society going swiftly to Gehenna. It is the entire absence of despair, bitterness, or cynicism in his work that gives it its altogether unique place in the history of social satire. Never before was there such a lenient barb on such a well-aimed arrow.

But if his business is not with the causes which contributed to the character of English Society in his time, it is with their effects. No satirist has ever put more highly representative figures on to his stage. They are so highly representative because they conform so strictly to type. He puts a valuation upon everyone whom he introduces on his stage. He shows exactly the regard in which we are to hold them and their profession. And it is interesting, in the light of the favour with which he always treated the typical *savant*, to hear from his son that he was always as much interested in what was being accomplished in science as in anything else in the world. We must conclude scientists were first in his estimation as men, from the pains he was at to give them the appearance of distinction in his pictures. Then he had much regard for Generals, great Admirals, and other magnificent specimens, the Adonis, for instance, that figures almost as often, and nearly always in company with, his charming woman. This gentleman is difficult to describe. He seems too languid even for the profession of man-about-town, but his clothes are such that one would think their irreproachability could only be maintained by a life of dedication to them. Did he ever exist? Du Maurier is very subtle here. He fully appreciated the great aim of the public-school-trained man in his own time—the elaborate care with which an officer studied to conceal an enthusiasm for the profession of arms, the great air of indolence with which over-work was concealed in the other fashionable professions. As a matter of fact these beautiful priests in the temple of "good form" were splendid stoics. They would lay it down that as long as correctness of attitude was maintained nothing mattered.

The artist seems to share many of the prejudices of the older aristocrats. He makes his Jews too Jewish. He believes that they produce great artists, and as if this wasn't enough, he still holds them at arm's length. We have in his art not only the record of social innovations, but a picture of the aristocrats before the barbarian invasion. As a picture of them then his art has now its value. And yet he was not quite an aristocrat in temperament, which is a little different from being one by birth. He would have been less tolerant of the Philistines if he had been, and more Bohemian too. He made his great excursions into Bohemia, but he reached it always by a journey through the suburbs. His love of glamour and enchantment was aristocratic, but he did not keep it to the end. He loses it in later drawings. His satire, too, grows less pointed after the eighties, with an equivalent decline in the art by which it is conveyed. The poetic vein that once distinguished him from the Society he depicted tended also to disappear, as he succumbed to a process of absorption into a Society which he had once been able to observe with the freshness of a stranger. It is familiarity that blunts our sense of beauty. It is in its last phase in *Punch* that his drawing loses the poetry that characterised it in the seventies and eighties, and which gave his satire then such a potent stealthy influence over those for whom it was intended.

ILLUSTRATION FOR "RECOLLECTIONS OF AN ENGLISH
GOLD-MINE" ONCE A WEEK, 1861.

§2

If it were possible to imagine a world without any women or children in it, du Maurier's contemporary, Keene, so far as we can judge from his art, would have got along very well in such a world. He would have missed the voluminous skirt that followed the crinoline, with its glorious opportunity for beautiful spacing of white in a drawing, more than he would have missed its wearer. But du Maurier's art is Romantic; in the background of its chivalric regard for women there is the history of the worship of the Virgin. The source of such an art would have to be sought for in the neighbourhood of Camelot. It is impossible to overlook the chivalry that will not allow him, except with pain, to make a woman ugly. He was first of all a Poet, and though it may be a man's business to put a poem on to paper, it is a woman's to create it. He was a poet put into the business of satire with sufficient wit to sustain himself there. Many a time he has to make the satire rest almost entirely with the legend at the foot of his drawing; by obscuring their legends we find that drawing after drawing has nothing to tell us but of the beauty of those involved in "the joke," and this, as we shall show further on, gives a peculiar salt, or rather sweetness, to satire from his pencil. He is a romancer. His dialogues are romances. It is the novelist and artist running side by side in the legend and the drawing, but almost independently of each other, the wit and the poet in him trying to play each other's game, that provides the contradictoriness—the charm in his pictures. The point of the "joke" seems very often a mere excuse for working off several incidents of beauty that have been perceived.

In dealing with *fashion* du Maurier scores with posterity. Beauty, when it really is recorded, is the one element in any transitory fashion that survives the challenge of time. It is natural for one generation to hate more than anything else in the world the fashions immediately preceding the one affected. Pointed contemporary satire has, from the very shape it must assume, an ephemeral success. It is only when something more than the mere object of the satire is involved by some grace of the satirist's genius—some response on his part to charm in the thing assailed, that the work of satire comes down from its own time with an indestructible ingredient in it.

As a record of feminine fashion du Maurier's drawings in *Punch* are remarkable. It must not be imagined that the history of fashion is merely the tale of dressmakers' caprice. The very language of changing ideals is the variation of the toilet. When women were restricted to an oriental extent within convention, when to be "prim" was the aim of life, no feature of dress was lacking that could put "abandonment" of any but a moral kind, out of the question. A shake of the head too quickly and the coiffure was imperilled; the movements that came within the prescribed circle of dignity within the circle of the crinoline were all of a rhythmical order. Women did not take to moving with freedom because the crinoline went out, but the crinoline went out when they took to moving with freedom. It went out simply because it was a confounded nuisance. It was a natural costume only as long as women imagined it was natural to them to be very still in demeanour. Once they began to have opinions about that matter they soon sent the crinoline on its way. The same process goes on with the fashions of wearing the hair. The Blue-stocking, constantly running her nervous fingers up her forehead into her hair, has given to Girton a style of its own, equivalent to none at all. *Fashion* is more sensible than most things. If it changes with a rapidity that dazzles man, is not that only because man is stupid?

To study hair-dressing in du Maurier's pictures, is to study the growth of the nineteenth-century woman's mind. The head-dress becomes more natural as woman herself becomes more natural. It becomes more Greek when she takes up the Amazon idea, and simple when she discards some of the complications of convention, always to return to elaboration in the winter when it is not easy to live the simple life after the bell goes for dinner.

When the crinoline went out the train came in; so that though woman had allowed *herself* more freedom, man could only walk behind her at a respectful distance with a ceremonial measure of pace. The dressmaker did not control all this; the resources of her transcendent art were strained to keep up with the march of womanhood—that was all. If we may believe du Maurier's art, the note of beauty never entirely disappeared from *fashion* until the æsthetic women of the eighties seemed to take in hand their own clothes. The æsthetic ladies failed, as the movement to which they attached themselves did, for beauty is something attendant upon life, arriving when it likes, going away very often when everyone is on his knees for it to remain.

§3

When it comes to his drawings of children du Maurier is very far away from the sentimentalist of the Barrie school. He does not attempt to go through the artifice of pretended possession of the realm of the child's mind. He was of those who find the curious attractiveness of childhood in the unreality, and not, as claimed by the later school, the superior reality of the child's world. His view of the child is the affectionate, but the "Olympian" one, with its amused appreciation of the *naïveté* and the charm of childhood's particular brand of self-possession. It is possible that his nursery scenes played some part in promoting the respect that is given to-day to the impulses of childhood, the enlightened and beautiful side of which respect after all so far outweighs the ridiculous and sentimental one. His nursery drawings contribute much of the fragrance associated with his work in *Punch*. He takes rank under the best definition of an artist, namely, one who can put his own values upon the things that come up for representation on his paper. By his insistence upon certain pleasant things he helped to establish them in the ideal, which, on the morrow, always tends to become the real. He was a realist only to the extent of their possibility. It gave him no pleasure whatever to enumerate, and represent over again, the many times in which the beautiful intentions of nature had gone astray. He liked to be upon the side of her successes. He constantly helped us to believe in, and to will towards the existence of such a world here on

8

earth, as we have set our heart upon. He is not an idealist in the vague sense, for he imports no beauty merely from dreamland. Like the Greeks, he makes *the possible* his single ideal. In insisting upon the possibility of beauty and suppressing every reference to the monstrous story of failure which the existence of hideousness implies, once more he puts the world in debt to art after the fashion of the old masters. For after all it seems to have been left for modern artists to grow wealthy and live comfortably upon the proceeds of their own relation of the world's despair; if they are playwrights, to live most snugly upon the box-receipts of an entrapped audience unnerved for the struggle of life by their ghastly picture of life's gloom.

However splendid the art in such a case we put it well down below that art which exerts the same amount of effort in trying to sustain the will to believe in, and so to bring about the reign of things we really want.

Du Maurier's art was nearer to reality, and not farther away, in the charming side of it. Realism does not necessarily imply only the representation of the mean and the defaulting. It is perhaps because humanity so passionately desires the reign of beauty that it is inclined to doubt that art which witnesses to the dream of it as already partly true.

Although du Maurier's art in its tenderness is romantic, in its belief in the ideal and in its insistence upon type rather than individuality it is Classic. In the fact that it is so it fails in intimacy of mood—just the intimacy that is the soul of Keene's art, which descends from Rembrandt's. But this point will come up for consideration farther on. Here it only concerns us in its connection with the psychology of the people it interprets in satire. There is the psychology of individuals and the psychology of a whole society—the latter was du Maurier's theme. It is generally an obsession, a "fad," a "craze," or "fashion" that his pencil exploits. He does not with Keene laugh with an individual at another individual. His art is well-bred in its style partly through the fact of its limitations. Moreover, in "Society" individuality tends to be less evident than amongst the poorer classes, with whom eccentricity is respected. In "Society" the force of individuality now runs beneath the surface of observable varieties of costume, taking a subterranean course with an impulse to avoid everything that would give rise to comment. But the conformity of "Society" in small things is only a mask. Du Maurier's real weakness in satire was that he did not quite perceive this. He was inclined to accept appearances for realities, with the consequence that the record he transmits of late Victorian Society obscures the quite feverish genius of that age.

§4

It has often been remarked that the comparative failure of du Maurier's successors seems the result of a difficulty in drawing "a lady" unmistakably. We can forgive much to the artist who brought the English lady, by many accounted the finest in the world, into real existence in modern comic art. We shall have to forgive him for turning into a lady every woman who was not middle-aged. Du Maurier's picture of Society was largely falsified by his inability to appreciate variety in feminine genius. But we are quite prepared to believe that his treatment of the dainty parlour-maid, for instance, helped to confirm that tradition of refinement in table service which is the pleasant feature of English home life. All the servants shown in his pictures are ladies, and this before the fashion had made any headway of engaging ladies as servants. And we cannot help feeling such delightful child-life as he represents could only have retained its characteristics under the wing of the beautiful women who nurse it in his pictures.

Both du Maurier and Keene knew the *genus* artist in all its varieties; and it is very interesting to contrast, and note the difference between, the "Artist" whom du Maurier brings into his society scenes and the one of Keene's drawings. In Keene's case the "artist" is generally a slouching Bohemian creature who belongs to a world of his own, and bears the stamp of "stranger" upon him in any other. But the "artist" of du Maurier, putting aside the æsthete coterie, with whom we shall deal presently, wears upon him every outward symbol of peace with the world—*The* world, Mayfair. He is always an "R.A."—symbol of respectability—whether du Maurier mentions it or not. With this type Art is one of the great recognised professions like The

Army or The Bar. We have no curiosity as to what sort of pictures they paint. We know that their art was suitable for the Academy, therefore for the Victorian Drawing-room. We are merely amused at the solemnity of manner with which they assumed that their large-sized Christmas cards had anything to do with art at all—cards which lost the purchasers of them such enormous sums when sold again at Christie's that the shaken confidence of the public as to the worth of modern pictures has not recovered to this day.

"THE CILICIAN PIRATES" THE CORNHILL, APRIL 1863.

All through this state of things, too, the really vital work of the time was left to the encouragement of those whom "Society" would then have called "outsiders," and it was just this failure on the part of the aristocracy to enlist the genius of the period on its own side that betrayed its decrepitude.

§5

The enduring feature of du Maurier's art, that which survives in it better than its sometimes scathing commentary upon a passing "craze," is his close representation of the air with which people seek to foil each other in conversation and conceal their own trepidations.

His "Social Agonies" are among the best of this series. If he does not lay stress upon individual character, he still remains the master draughtsman of a state of mind. He succeeds thus in the very field where probably all that is most important in modern art, whether of the novel or of illustration, will be found.

Behind the economy of word and gesture in the conversational method of to-day there lies the history of the long struggle of the race through volubility to refinement of expression. Du Maurier's *Punch* pictures take their place in the field of psychology in which the modern novel has secured its greatest results, and the best appreciation of his *Punch* work was written in the eighties by Mr. Henry James, the supreme master in this field; the master of suspenses that are greater than the conversations in which they happen; the explorer of twilights of consciousness in which little passions contend.

The Society du Maurier depicted held its position upon more comfortable terms than any preceding it in history. It did not have, on the one hand, to trim to a court party, or, on the other, to concede anything to the people to keep itself in power. Yet it was as swollen with pride in its position as any society has ever been. The industrial phenomena of the age had suddenly filled its pockets; and it had nothing else in the world to do but to blow itself out with pride. But a Society holding its position without an effort of some kind of its own is bound to lose in character, and the confession of all the best literature of this time was of the baffled search for the soul of the prosperous class.

§6

For the appreciation of the artist's management of dialogue we must move for a page or two in Mrs. de Tomkyns' circle with Miss Lyon Hunter, Sir Gorgius Midas the Plutocrat, Sir Pompey Bedel (of Bedel, Flunke & Co.) the successful professional man, and the rest of the whole set, who understand each other in the freemasonry of a common ambition to get into another set.

Mamma. "Enfin, my love! We're well out of this! *What* a gang!!! Where shall we go next?"

Daughter. "To Lady Oscar Talbot's, Mamma."

Mamma. "She *snubs* one so I really can't *bear* it! Let us go to Mrs. Ponsonby de Tomkyns. It's just as select (except the Host and Hostess) and quite as amusing."

Daughter. "But Mrs. Tomkyns snubs one worse than Lady Oscar, Mamma!"

Mamma. "Pooh, my love! who cares for the snubs of a Mrs. Ponsonby de Tomkyns I should like to know, so long as she's clever enough to get the right people."

This is the conversation in the hall between two ladies leaving a party in one of du Maurier's most characteristic drawings. On every side there are footmen and a crowd of guests cloaking and departing. Of Mrs. Ponsonby de Tomkyns Mr. Henry James has said: "This lady is a real creation.... She is not one of the heroines of the æsthetic movement, though we may be sure she dabbles in that movement so far as it pays to do so. Mrs. Ponsonby de Tomkyns is a little of everything, in so far as anything pays. She is always on the look-out; she never misses an opportunity. She is not a specialist, for that cuts off too many opportunities, and the æsthetic people have the *tort* as the French say, to be specialists. No, Mrs. Ponsonby de Tomkyns is—what shall we call her?—well, she is the modern social spirit. She is prepared for everything; she is ready to take advantage of everything; she would invite Mr. Bradlaugh to dinner if she thought the Duchess would come to meet him. The Duchess is her great achievement—she never lets go of her Duchess. She is young, very nice-looking, slim, graceful, indefatigable. She tires poor Ponsonby completely out; she can keep going for hours after poor Ponsonby is reduced to stupefaction. This unfortunate husband is indeed almost stupefied. He is not, like his wife, a person of imagination. She leaves him far behind, though he is so inconvertible that if she were a less superior person he would have been a sad encumbrance. He always figures in the corner of the scenes in which she distinguishes herself, separated from her by something like the gulf that separated Caliban from Ariel. He has his hands in his pockets, his head poked forward; what is going on is quite beyond his comprehension. He vaguely wonders what his wife will do next;

her manoeuvres quite transcend him. Mrs. Ponsonby de Tomkyns always succeeds. She is never at fault; she is as quick as the instinct of self-preservation. She is the little London lady who is determined to be a greater one—she pushes, gently but firmly—always pushes. At last she arrives."

We have quoted this delightful picture almost in its entirety from the essay upon du Maurier written by Mr. Henry James in the eighties to which we have referred. It describes the type of woman revealed in Mrs. de Tomkyns when we have followed her adventures up a little way in the back numbers of *Punch*. But, if we may be permitted the slang, the type itself is anything but "a back number." Du Maurier's work bids fair to live in the enjoyment of many generations, from the fact that its chaff, for the most part, is directed against vanities that recur in human nature. Mr. James tells us that the lady of whom we write "hesitates at nothing; she is very modern. If she doesn't take the æsthetic line more than is necessary, she finds it necessary to take it a little; for if we are to believe du Maurier, the passion for strange raiment and blue china has during the last few years made ravages in the London world." Mr. Henry James himself is one of the experts of the London world. There is almost a hint in the last sentence that he thought du Maurier's genius helped to nurse the crazes it made fun of.

Since writing this I have been told by one to whom du Maurier related the incident, that the hero of the æsthetic movement himself, Oscar Wilde, offered to sit to du Maurier for the chief character in his skit. Wilde was very young, but already master of that art of self-advertisement which he received from Byron and Disraeli, perfected, and, I think, handed on to Mr. Bernard Shaw. But such anxiety for every kind of celebrity at any cost seems to have lost the youthful genius the esteem of the great *Punch* artist once and for all. The representative of humorous journalism seems the one upon whom the delicate humour of the proposal was lost.

As far as du Maurier was capable of vindictiveness it was reserved for Maudle and Postlethwaite. He went out of his way to give a contemptible appearance to those who took the name of Art in vain. His only spiteful drawings are those of æsthetes. They are spiteful to the extent of the great disgust which he, the most amiable of satirists, felt for them. But still he was careful not to treat a craze which afforded him inexhaustible variations of subject matter with so much bitterness as to kill it right out. It was only towards this craze that he showed any bitterness at all, for the rest he is always amused with Society. He has none of the bitter Jeremiahlike anger against it of a Swift.

Mr. Henry James defending du Maurier from a charge of being malignant, brought against him for his ugly representation of queer people, failures, and grotesques, refused to allow that the taint of "French ferocity" of which the artist was accused, existed. But Mr. Henry James sees in du Maurier's ugly people a real specification of type, where we confess that we have felt that his "ferocity" missed the point of resemblance to type through clumsy exaggeration. One noticeable instance, however, to our mind, where the too frequent outrageousness is replaced by an exquisite study of character, is in the face of the fair authoress who, when the gallant Colonel, anxious to break the ice, and full of the fact that he has just been made a proud father, asks if she takes any interest in very young children, replies, "I loathe *all* children!" (January 13, 1880).

ILLUSTRATION FOR "WIVES AND DAUGHTERS" THE CORNHILL, 1864.

§7

The story of children's conversation has perhaps never been told quite so charmingly as du Maurier tells it. We could quote endlessly from the admirably constructed nursery dialogues in which he does not attempt to make a joke, and in which he very carefully refrains from giving a fantastic precocity to his little characters—dialogues in which he is quite content to rely upon our sympathetic knowledge of children's way of putting things, while he rests the appeal of the drawing and legend entirely upon a *naïve* literalness to their remarks. The charming atmosphere of the well-ordered nursery must be felt by readers, and then we can quote from the text of some of his drawings of the kind; this we shall do somewhat at random and as they come to mind.

"Are you asleep, dearest? Yes, Mamma, and the Doctor particularly said that I wasn't to be waked to take my medicine" (*July* 10, 1880).

"Oh, Auntie! There's your tiresome cook's been and filled my egg too full" (*April* 22, 1882).

Already we are seized with misgivings as to whether, with the reader very much on the look-out for the jokes, we shall be successful in making our point in claiming for du Maurier that, as much as any author who has ever written upon children, he captures "the note" of children's speeches. But anyhow we will try.

For an instance there is the delightful picture of a child clasping its mother round the knees, whilst the mother, shawled for an evening concert, bends affectionately down—

"Good Night! Good Night! my dear, sweet, pretty mamma! I like you to go out, because if you didn't you'd never come home again, you know."

The artist perhaps invented this pretty speech, but the "Good Night! Good Night! my dear, sweet, pretty mamma" is of the very spirit of the redundancy by which children hope in heaping words together to express accumulation of emotion. Du Maurier's children never make the nasty pert answers upon which, for their nearly impossible but always vulgar smartness, the providers of jokes about children for the comic papers generally depend. He is simply going on with his "novel" — *The Tale of the House* it might be called — when he affords us realistic glimpses of nursery conversation.

Mamma. "What is Baby crying for, Maggie?"

Maggie. "I don't know."

Mamma. "And what are you looking so indignant about?"

Maggie. "That nasty, greedy dog's been and took and eaten my punge-take!"

Mamma. "Why, I saw you eating a sponge-cake a minute ago!"

Maggie. "O — that was Baby's."

We need hardly labour the point of the "been and took and eaten" as an instance of felicity in reconstructing children's conversation, and making the verisimilitude to their grammar the charm of the reconstruction.

Ethel. "Isn't it sad, Arthur? There's the drawing-room cleared for a dance, and all the dolls ready to begin, only they've got no partners!"

Arthur. "Well, Ethel! There's the four gentlemen in my Noah's Ark; but they don't look as if they cared very much about *dancing*, you know!" (*February* 24, 1872).

Ethel. "And O, Mamma, do you know as we were coming along we saw a horrid woman with a red striped shawl drink something out of a bottle, and then hand it to some men. I'm sure she was tipsy."

Beatrice (who always looks on the best side of things). "Perhaps it was only Castor Oil, after all!"

A whispered appeal. "Mamma! Mamma! don't scold him any more, it makes the room so dark."

It is the *poetry* of the nursery that is to be felt throughout du Maurier's art in this vein. And how well he knows the emotions of childhood. For instance, the large drawing "Farewell to Fair

Normandy" (October 2, 1880), extending across two full pages of *Punch*, in which the children away for their seaside holiday leave the sands for the last time in a mournful procession. The sky is dimmed with an evening cloud. Du Maurier has compressed much poetry into the scene. It has been said that "there is only one art," and this seems to be proved on great occasions by those who can command more than one art for the expression of their feelings. It is difficult to say where in this picture the artist in du Maurier gives place to the poet, as difficult as it is to say before a picture of Rossetti.

ILLUSTRATION FOR "WIVES AND DAUGHTERS" THE CORNHILL, 1865.

Sometimes du Maurier even depicted delightful children as the victims of the fashionable crazes that he loved to attack, and thus we are brought to another series of dialogues—as a rule though only involving the "grown-ups"—in which the legend and the type of person depicted, together, form a most valuable document of the times. There is for instance the China mania—in the following in the incipient stage:—

"O Mamma! O! O! N—N—Nurse has given me my C—C—Cod-liver Oil out of a p—p—plain white mug" (*December* 26, 1874).

Then the inimitable colloquies of the æsthetes—and especially the now famous one about the six-mark tea-pot.

Aesthetic Bridegroom. "It is quite consummate, is it not?"

Intense Bride. "It is, indeed! Oh, Algernon, let us live up to it!"

Also the direction, to the architect about the country house:

Fair Client. "I want it to be nice and baronial, Queen Anne and Elizabethan, and all that; kind of quaint and Nuremburgy you know—regular Old English, with French windows opening to the lawn, and Venetian blinds, and sort of Swiss balconies, and a loggia. But I'm sure *you* know what I mean!" (*November* 29, 1890).

And farther on in the *Punch* volumes:—

"O, Mr. Robinson, does not it ever strike you, in listening to sweet music, that the Rudiment of Potential Infinite Pain is subtly woven into the tissue of our keenest joy" (*December* 2, 1891).

But perhaps before closing this chapter we should give some examples of drawing-room conversation pure and simple, without reference to any sort of craze, as specimens of their author's skill. Familiarity with the artist's characters will enable the reader to appreciate the note of a shy man's agony in some, and of feminine spite in others.

Among the "Speeches to be lived down, if possible," there are these:

She. "Let me introduce you to a very charming lady, to take down to supper."

He. "A—thanks—no. I never eat supper."

"By George! I am so hungry I can't talk."

Fair Hostess (on hospitable thoughts intent). "Oh, I'm so glad!"

"Things one would rather have left unsaid":

Amiable Hostess. "What! must you go already? Really, Professor, it's too bad of this sweet young wife of yours to carry you off so early! She always does!"

Professor. "No, no, not *always*, Mrs. Bright. At *most* houses I positively have to drag her away!"

"Truths that might have been left unspoken":

Hostess. "What? haven't you brought your sisters, Mr. Jones?"

Mr. Jones. "No, they couldn't come, Mrs. Smith. The fact is, they're saving themselves for Mrs. Brown's Dance to-morrow, you know!" (*January* 9, 1886).

Under the heading "Feline Amenities":

Fair Hostess (to Mrs. Masham, who is looking her very best). "How-dy-do, dear? I hope you're not so tired as you look!"

Sympathetic Lady Guest. "Don't be unhappy about the rain, dear Mrs. Bounderson—it will soon be over, and your garden will be lovelier than ever."

Little Mrs. Goldmore Bounderson (who is giving her first Garden Party). "Yes; but I'm afraid it will keep my most desirable guests from coming!"

This last duologue is pure du Maurier. It is subtle.

"Feline Amenities" again:

"How kind of you to call—I'm sorry to have kept you waiting!"

"Oh, don't mention it.—I've not been at all bored! I've been trying to imagine what I should do to make this room look comfortable if it were mine!" (*November* 22, 1892).

The "Things one would rather have expressed otherwise" is a good series too:

The Professor (to Hostess). "Thank you so much for a most delightful evening! I shall indeed go to bed with pleasant recollections—and *you* will be the very *last* person I shall think of!"

And again, of the same series:

Fair Hostess. "Good-night, Major Jones. We're supposed to breakfast at nine, but we're not very punctual people. Indeed the later you appear to-morrow morning, the better pleased we shall all be" (*May* 13, 1893).

"Things one would rather have left unsaid":

He. "Yes, I know Bootle slightly, and confess I don't think much of him!"

She. "I know him a little too. He took me in to dinner a little while ago!"

He. "Ah, that's just about all he's fit for!"

The Hostess. "Dear Miss Linnet! would you—would you sing one of those charming ballads, while I go and see if supper's ready?"

The Companion. "O, don't ask me—I feel nervous. There are so many people."

The Hostess. "O, they won't listen, bless you! not one of them! *Now* DO!!!"

And here is a conversation that betrays the presence of one of the currents of public feeling below the smooth surface of well-bred twaddle:

In the Metropolitan Railway. "I beg your pardon, but I think I had the pleasure of meeting you in Rome last year?"

"No, I've never been nearer to Rome than St. Alban's."

"St. Alban's? Where is that?"

"Holborn."

Some rather amusing speeches of a different character in which du Maurier assails the more obvious forms of snobbery of a class below those with whom his art was generally concerned may be given:

Among the Philistines. Grigsby. "Do you *know* the Joneses, Mrs. Brown?"

"No, we—er—don't care to know *Business* people as a rule, although my husband's in business; but then he's in the *Coffee* Business and they're all *gentlemen* in the *Coffee* Business, you know!"

Grigsby (who always suits himself to his company). "*Really* now! Why, that's more than can be said of the Army, the Navy, the Church, the Bar, or even the *House of Lords*! I don't *wonder* at your being rather *exclusive*!" (*Punch's Almanac*, 1882).

"I see your servants wear cockades now, Miss Shoddson!"

"Yes, Pa's just become a member of the Army and Navy Stores."

When du Maurier confined himself to observing and to recording he never failed for subjects. But we suppose as a concession to a section of the public he felt a leaven of mere jokes was demanded from him every year. The scene of his struggle to invent those "jokes" is one to be veiled. It is safe to say that it is his distinction to have contributed at once the best satire and the worst jokes that *Punch* has ever published. A black and white artist has told the writer that the *Art-Editors* of papers look first at the joke. The drawing is accepted or rejected on the joke. We can only be glad that this was not entirely the editorial practice on *Punch* in du Maurier's time. Perhaps the subjoined "joke" of du Maurier's from *Punch* is the worst in the world:

"I say, cousin Constance, I've found out why you always call your Mamma 'Mater.'"

"Why, Guy?"

"Because she's always trying to find a mate for you girls."

SKETCH FOR ILLUSTRATION FOR "WIVES AND DAUGHTERS"
1865.

And yet if the drawing accompanying this joke be looked at *first*, it delights with its charm and distinction. Here then is a psychological fact; the drawing itself seems to the eye a poorer affair once the poor joke has been read. Having suffered in this way several times in following with admiration the pencil of du Maurier through the old volumes of *Punch*, we at last hit upon the plan of always covering the joke and enjoying first the picture for its own sake, only uncovering the legend when this has been thoroughly appreciated lest it should turn out to be merely a feeble joke instead of a happily-invented conversation. There are some of the drawings for jokes which we should very much like to have included with our illustrations, but the human mind being so constituted that it goes direct to the legend of an illustration, feeling "sold" if it isn't there, and the "jokes" in some of these instances being so fatal to the understanding of the atmosphere and charm of the drawing, we have had to abandon the idea of doing so. What the reader has to understand is that circumstances harnessed du Maurier to a certain business; he imported all manner of extraneous graces into it, and thus gave a determination to the character of the art of satire which it will never lose. The pages of *Punch* were enriched, beautified, and made more delicately human. *Punch* gained everything through the connection and du Maurier a stimulus in the demand for regular work. But it is not impossible to imagine circumstances which, but for this early connection with *Punch*, would have awakened and developed a different and perhaps profounder side of du Maurier, of which we seem to get a glimpse in the illustrations to Meredith in *The Cornhill Magazine*.

§8

The famous reply of an early Editor to the usual complaint that *Punch* was not as good as it used to be—"No, sir, it never was"—cannot be considered to hold good in any comparison between the present period and that in which the arts of du Maurier and Keene held sway. There have been periods, there is such a one now, when the literary side of *Punch* has touched a high-water mark. But on the illustrative side *Punch* seems to be always hoping that another Keene or du Maurier will turn up. It does not seem prepared to accept work in quite another style. But there is no more chance of there ever being another Keene than of there being another Rembrandt, or of there ever being another du Maurier than another Watteau. The next genius to whom it is given to illuminate the pages of the classic journal in a style that will rival the past is not likely to arise from among those who think that there is no other view of life than that which was discovered by their immediate predecessors. By force of his genius—or, if you prefer it, of sympathy—which means the same thing—for some particular phase of life, some artist may at any moment uncover in its pages an altogether fresh kind of humour and of beauty.

§ 9

Du Maurier's art covers the period when England was flushed with success. Artists in such times grow wealthy, and by their work refine their time. But in spite of the number of wealthy Academicians living upon Society in the mid-Victorian time, the influence of Art upon Society was less than at any time in history in which circumstances have been favourable to the artist.

The great wave of trade that carried the shop-keeper into the West-end drawing-room strewed also the curtains and carpets with that outrageous weed of *trade* design which gave to the mid-Victorian world its complexion of singular hideousness.

The æsthetic movement indicated the restlessness of some of the brighter spirits with this condition, but many of its remedies were worse than the disease. The *nouveau* artist-craftsman stood less chance than anybody of getting back to the secret of noble things, having forsaken the path of pure utility which, wherever it may go for a time, always leads back again to beauty. The disappearance of beauty for a time need not have been a cause of despair. Beauty will always come back if it is left alone. People had been swept off their feet with delight at what machinery could do, and they expected beauty to come out of it as a product at the same pace as everything else. It was not a mistake to expect it from any source, but from this particular source it could only come with time. There is evidence that it is on the way. And yet though the results of crude mechanical industrialism spoilt the outward appearance of the whole of the Victorian age, the earlier part at least of that time was one of marked personal refinement. We have but to look at portraits by George Richmond and others to receive a great impression of distinction. And this fact enables us to throw into clearer light the exact nature of du Maurier's work. If we seek for evidence in the old volumes of *Punch* for the distinction of the early Victorians we shall not find it.

We shall merely conceive instead a dislike for the type of gentleman of the time. Leech and his contemporaries did nothing more for their age than to make it look ridiculous for ever. But du Maurier gives us a real impression of the Society in which he moved. His ability to satirise society while still leaving it its dignity is unique. It may be said to be his distinctive contribution to the art of graphic satire. It gave to the Anglo-Saxon school its present-day characteristic, putting upon one of the very lightest forms of art the stamp of a noble time. The point is that whilst du Maurier thus deferred to the dignity of human nature he remained a satirist, not a humorist merely, as was Keene.

II

THE ART OF DU MAURIER

§ 1

If we wish to estimate the art of du Maurier at its full worth we must try and imagine *Punch* from 1863 without this art, and try for a moment to conceive the difference this absence would make to our own present knowledge of the Victorians; also to the picture always entertained of England abroad.

If we are to believe du Maurier's art England is a petticoat-governed country. The men in his pictures are often made to recede into the background of Victorian ornament merely as ornaments themselves. As for the women, the mask of manner, the pleasantness concealing every shade of uncharitableness, all the arts of the contention for social precedence—in the interpretation of this sort of thing du Maurier is often quite uncanny, but he is never ruthless.

We have noticed that when du Maurier tried to draw ugly people he often only succeeded in turning out a figure of fun. Not to be beautiful and charming is to fail of being human, seems the judgment of his pencil. This was his limitation. And another was that, whilst professing to be concerned with humanity as a whole, he nearly always broke down with types that outraged the polite standard. He was a master in the description of Bishops and Curates, Generals and Men-about-town, but he broke down when he came to "the out-sider." And, as we have already pointed out, he seldom got away from types to individuals.

In the last respect, however, we gain more perhaps than we lose. We gain a very vivid impression of the whole tone of the society in his time. And the fact of his art passing over the individual, for ever prevented it from cruelty, for to be cruel the individual must be hit. He did not satirise humanity, but Society. And his criticism was not of its members, but of its ways. Except in the case of children, he left unrevealed the individual heart that Keene so sympathetically exposed.

He made an original—and who will deny it?—a unique contribution to the history of satire, when he went to work through literalness and care for beauty in a field where nearly all previous success had rested with a sort of ruffianism. But chiefly one praises Heaven for the nurseryful of delightful children he let loose in his pages against the army of little monsters who reign as children in the Comic Press, bearing witness as they do to the unpleasant kind of mind even an artist can possess.

Though he ridiculed "Camelot," his own tradition, as we have shown, was received from the Arthurian source. His chivalry gave his satire a very delicate edge. It was infinitely more cutting in showing the misfit of vulgarity with beauty than in showing vulgarity alone.

But du Maurier's gentlemanliness narrowed his range. It forced him into putting down something preposterous instead of a true type as soon as he wished to create "a bounder." He found it impossible to get inside of a "bounder"—to be for the time a "bounder" himself. It is necessary for an artist to be able to be every character that he would create. And perhaps a satirist never wounds others so much as when he most wounds himself. Thackeray succeeded with snobbery because he had enough of it to go on with himself. We have shown the success of du Maurier with the æsthetes to go upon similar lines. The soul of satire is very often the bitterness of confession. In his very style the satirist of the æsthetes stood confessed almost as one of their number, whether he wished this to be seen or not—at least as one of the romantic school from whom they immediately descended. But he was genuine; where Postlethwaite and Maudle posed, his irritation was with the pose, the pretended preoccupation with beauty. He genuinely admired the Florentine revival, and to admire is to be jealous of those who take in vain. He wished to show up the "æsthetes" as the parasites they were, trading socially upon an inspiration too fragrant to be traded with at all.

Du Maurier, who assuredly knew what elegance was as well as any man of his time, took a great delight in pointing out to all whom it might concern, by illustration, that if there was any beauty of representation possible to him, as an artist, in depicting modern society, it was not in anything put forward in the shape of costume by the ladies of the æsthetic movement, but in the unacknowledged genius of ordinary dressmakers.

It was in his time that Philistinism met its match in Oscar Wilde, and for the first time in its history felt its self-complacency shaken. Up to that time it had been very proud of itself. With the loss of that pride it blundered, and it remained for du Maurier to show that the height of Philistinism in a Philistine is to pretend not to be a Philistine.

He had always seen what it would do present-day Londoners a world of good to see as clearly, that it is just those who affect, and who, by their lack of artistic constitution, are incapable of doing more than merely affecting, the understanding of art, who are the worst enemies it has in the world. He preferred the open Philistine. And so do we. The affectation described lends to art an artificial support which betrays those who attempt to rest any scheme for the promotion of art upon it.

But though du Maurier was not a Philistine he had the genius of respectability. His pencil could get on well with Bishops. It is easy enough to put a model into a Bishop's apron and gaiters, but that does not secure the drawing of a Bishop. It is necessary to observe that du Maurier found definite lines with his pencil for something so abstract as Broad-Churchmanship. The High-Churchman, with his perilous inclination to fervour, he was afraid of as a disturbing element, and kept him out of his drawings.

§2

We have noted that it was du Maurier's peculiar genius to respond to "attainment" in life, even as the Greeks did, rather than to life's pathetic and romantic struggle. Du Maurier, we believe, was of opinion that if circumstances—he probably meant Editorial ones—had determined that he should apply his art to the lower classes he would have succeeded as well there as he did with Society. We prefer to believe that the Editorial instinct in the direction it gave to his work knew better. Many opportunities were afforded him for being as democratic in spirit as he liked, but he left such opportunities alone. His cab-runners run about in rain-shrunken suits that were obviously made in Savile Row; everyone of them, they are broken-down gentlemen. Coachmen, gardeners, footmen, pages, housekeepers, cooks, ladies' maids, and all those who move in the domestic circle of the upper classes he could draw, but his taste in life is a marked one, and that means it is a limited one. It is as marked as Meredith's, and it is much of the same kind; like that writer's great lady, Mrs. Mountstuart Jenkinson, he preferred persons "that shone in the sun." This had nothing whatever to do with qualities of the heart; it was all an æsthetic predilection. The moment his pencil touched the theme of life lived upon as gentle a plane as possible, then something was kindled at its point which betrayed the presence of genuine inspiration. The inspiration was of the same nature as Watteau's, the grace of a certain aspect of life making an æsthetic appeal. Let this attraction to what is gracious in appearance, however, be kept distinct from the effect made by the spectacle of wealth upon the snob. Those who show us the beauty in the world, enrich the world with that much of beauty.

PENCIL STUDIES FROM THE ARTIST'S SKETCH BOOK

In his *Life and Letters of Charles Keene*, Mr. G.S. Layard[1] says this:—

"That Keene could have drawn the lovely be-Worthed young ladies and the splendidly proportioned and frock-coated young men with which Mr. du Maurier delights us week by week, not to speak of the god-like hero of his charming novel, I do not think anyone can doubt, had he set himself to do it, but it was part of the ineradicable Bohemianism of his character and the realistic bent of his genius that made him shun the representation of what he considered artificial and an outrage upon nature."

This, it will perhaps be admitted, is not very good art-criticism. Though in justice to its author it must be said that he did not wish to be regarded as Keene's critic as well as biographer.

An artist does not argue with himself that he will shun the representation of one particular side of life. He simply leaves it alone because he cannot help it; it does not attract him. He draws just that which interests him most and in the way in which it interests him; and exactly to the measure of his interest does his drawing possess vitality. Keene might have expressed with pungency his sense of certain things as being artificial and outrageous, but as long as his feelings towards them remained like that he could not express himself about them in any other way, certainly not in du Maurier's way—that is, with du Maurier's skill.

To the extent to which there *is* a glamour and a beauty in fashion du Maurier is a realist. People who only now and then become sensible of the charm in things are provoked by its strangeness in art, and call it romance, their definition for an untrue thing.

§3

During the period of thirty-six years over which du Maurier contributed to *Punch* the paper took upon itself a character unlike anything that had preceded it in comic journalism; it created a tradition for itself which placed it beside *The Times*—the "Thunderer," as one of the institutions of this country, recognised abroad as essentially expressive of national character. English humour, like American and French, has its own flavour; it lacks the high and extravagant fantasy that is so exhilarating in America; it avoids the subtlety of France; it is essentially a laughing humour. The Englishman, who cannot stand chaff himself, always laughs at others. It is curious that while an Englishman's conventions rest upon dislike of what is odd and fantastic—precisely the two most well-known sources of humour—he yet has a sense of humour. The first aim of every Englishman is to acquire a manner of some dignity. It is the breaking down of that dignity in other people that to his eyes places them in a light that is funny.

English humour seems to find its object in physical rather than mental aspects. The very notable feature of du Maurier's work was that it refined upon the characteristics of English humour; it dealt always with people placed by an absurd speech, or an unlucky gesture, in a foolish position—a position the shy distress of which was a physical experience. Du Maurier's humour was also English in its kindness; the points that are scored against the unfortunate object of it are the points that may be scored against the laugher himself to-morrow. His pictures were a running commentary upon the refinements of our manners and upon the quick changes of moral costume that fresh situations in the social comedy demand.

One thing peculiarly fitted the artist to be the satirist of English Society—his love of the comedy of people by nature honest finding themselves only able to get through the day with decent politeness by the aid of "the lie to follow." English people, Puritan by ancestry and by inclination, are nevertheless driven into frequent subterfuge by their good nature, and having pared their language and gesture of that extravagance in expression which they despise in the foreigner, they are thrown back upon a naturalness that betrays them in delicate situations. The consequence is that it is in Anglo-Saxon Society at its best that the art of delicate fence in conversation has been brought to its highest pitch. There the *clairvoyance* is so great that words can be used economically in relation to the realities of life, and are consequently often adopted merely as a screen before the feelings.

We have to realise how much more than any one preceding him in graphic satire du Maurier was able to dispense with exaggeration. Nevertheless, the studied avoidance of exaggeration has not had the happiest effect as a precedent in the art of *Punch*. Without du Maurier's sensitive response to the whole comedy of drawing-room life the tendency has been to lapse into the merely photographic.

The similitude we have already described between du Maurier's art with the pencil and the art of the modern novel is not complete until we have extended it further in the direction of a comparison with novels of George Meredith and Henry James in particular. Like these two writers du Maurier loved comedy, and your appreciator of comedy cannot stand the presence of a "funny man." In the pages of *Punch* it was Leech and not du Maurier who first replaced the art of the merely "funny man." He began with the pencil the kind of art that would answer to Meredith's description of the comic muse. Throughout *The Egoist*, by George Meredith, a comedy in which Clara Middleton's life comes near to being tragic, the air would clear at any moment if Sir Willoughby and Clara had not both lost through over-civilisation the power of saying precisely what they mean. The book is the story of how Clara tries to find words, and of how, when she finds them, the conversational genius of Willoughby seemingly deflects them from the meaning she intends them to bear. It was in the mid-region between two people in conversation where false constructions are put by either party upon what is said that du Maurier, like Meredith himself, perceived the source of comedy was to be found.

§4

We have already defined the drawing-room as a Victorian institution. It belonged to an age that was willing to sacrifice too much to appearances—one in which everyone seemed to live for appearances. It was a sort of stage, occupied by people in afternoon or evening costume, with even the chairs arranged, not where they were wanted, but where they made a good appearance. Oscar Wilde suggested to the Victorians that they shouldn't *arrange* chairs; they should let them occur. Against the false setting manners were bound to become false—good manners becoming almost synonymous with perfect insincerity. Perhaps the only thing that ever really came to life in a drawing-room was the æsthetic movement! At its worst it was what we have described it; at its best it was a sort of blind protest against the patterns of chair-covers that the eye was bound to absorb while listening to the inanities of drawing-room conversation. It is significant that the æsthetic movement was a man's movement. Until the leader of the movement appeared on the scene, the decoration of the Victorian, as distinct from the Georgian parlour, or that of every other period, was woman's business. Most of the Victorian patterns embodied naturalistic and sentimental representations of flowers. It was with the disappearance of the eighteenth-century tradition, when drawing-room decoration passed out of the hands of men, that beauty disappeared. Women took to heaping masses of drapery on to the mantelpieces which had once displayed classic proportion; on to this drapery they pinned all sorts of horrible fans. Du Maurier exposed it all, and he exposed, too, the æsthetes to whom the salvation of the appearance of a suburban drawing-room could come to mean more than anything else in life. Their fault was not confined to this. He always brought their "intensity" as a charge against them, for it is of the very genius of good manners to merely froth about things which, if taken seriously, would tend to destroy amenity.

ILLUSTRATION FOR "A LEGEND OF CAMELOT" — PART III.
PUNCH, MARCH 17, 1866.

A little castle she drew nigh,
With seven towers twelve inches high....
O Miserie!

A baby castle, all a-flame
With many a flower that hath no name,
O Miserie!

It had a little moat all round:
A little drawbridge too she found;
O Miserie!

On which there stood a stately maid,
Like her in radiant locks arrayed....
O Miserie!

Save that her locks grew rank and wild,
By weaver's shuttle undefiled!...
O Miserie!

Who held her brush and comb, as if
Her faltering hands had waxed stiff,
O Miserie!

With baulkt endeavour! whence she sung
A chant, the burden whereof rung:
O Miserie!

"These hands have striven in vain
To part
These locks that won GAUWAINE
His heart!"

It is interesting, as an addition to the comparison we have drawn
between Meredith and du Maurier, to note that of the illustrators to
Meredith's own novels it was the latter who seemed to experience
life in a mood similar to the author's. In illustrating *Harry Richmond*
he secured the Meredithian sense of romance and of pedigree in
scenes as well as people. However modern Meredith's characters
were, they were all the children of old-fashioned people; within
them all was the pride of the family tree, and, in the scenes in which
they move, the memory of an older world. Du Maurier, too, in his art

was a patrician, and when he gave up romance and took to satire pure and simple he put both beauty and dignity into the world that he described. All the time he was drawing his Society world others were working the same vein. But to him alone it seemed to be given to glimpse the splendour of it, and to suggest the link of romance that holds the present and the past together.

Let us praise that very wise Editor who, appreciating the artist's character, confined him to the art most natural to him. What has become of Editors of this kind to-day? Is not this the very genius of the art of editing—this and not the wholly fictitious "what the public wants?" Who knows what the public want but the public themselves? It is the artist who is allowed by his Editor to go his own way, who takes the public with him. If he has not the same sympathies as the public no Editorial direction will save the situation, while it will drive perhaps a fine artist away to another trade.

§ 5

After the appearance of his first drawing in *Punch*, for more than a year du Maurier's connection with the paper seems to have been maintained by the execution of initial letters for it. Mr. W.L. Bradbury, zealous in the preservation of all records that redound to the glory of *Punch*, has in one or two instances had pulls taken from the wood blocks upon special paper. These special proofs show all the charm of wood engraving. In the case of the initial large C, reproduced below, Mr. Bradbury's specimen shows the beautiful quality which in our own time Mr. Sturge Moore and Mr. Pissarro are at such pains to secure in engravings made for love of the art. One only wishes that the exigencies of book-production would allow us to attempt rivalry with Mr. Bradbury's specimen in our reproduction. But we see no reason why specimens of the wood-printing of du Maurier's work should not be on view in the British Museum. The "impressions" in old volumes of *Punch*, after the wear and tear, the opening and the shutting, and the effect of time are not an adequate record of du Maurier's skill in accommodating his art to the methods of reproduction of the period.

Moreover, du Maurier was better in securing an effect of painting than of pure line work with his pen. It is just this effect which suited the methods of engraving better than those of "process" work. And because it demanded drawing to a smaller scale, with lines closer together, the demands of engraving suited the nature of du Maurier's art better than those of "process" work.

When the modern process came in artists enlarged their drawings so as to secure delicacy of effect from the result of the reduction in printing. In such a case they really work for the sake of a result upon the printed page, and there is consequently less value to be attached to the original drawing. It generally errs on the side of coarseness. And now that a trade is driven in original drawings, artists are tempted to give the purchaser as much in the matter of size for his money as he may want. And, alas, it is true that many picture buyers do buy according to measurement, or anything else on earth rather than merit.

Du Maurier could add a reason of his own for availing himself of the opportunity to enlarge his drawings when he could, namely, that of his weak sight. But it is certainly not among the large drawings that we should look for the work that places him in the place we wish to claim for him.

It will well repay the student of du Maurier's art to look into the illustration for the novel *Wives and Daughters* reproduced above. In this very highly finished picture the drawing of all the detail seems done with the greatest pleasure to the artist. It has not the breadth of style which du Maurier himself could admire in Keene, but the line work is intensely sympathetic throughout; there is that enjoyment in the actual touch of pen to paper which was always characteristic of Keene, which is always special to great art; which, alas, was not always characteristic of du Maurier. It is like the touch of a sympathetic musician. Du Maurier, always generous to his contemporaries, in his lecture upon art, instances the natural skill of Walker by his success with the difficulties of drawing a tall hat. But Walker himself has nothing of this kind better to show than the hat in the picture we are describing.

§6

In the early eighties the change was made from drawing on wood to drawing on paper for *Punch*, the drawing being afterwards photographed on to the wood. Later, metal was made possible as a substitute for wood, and this enabled illustrations and letterpress to be printed together. The modern process of reproduction has introduced its own pleasant qualities into journalism, and because they are different in effect they do not rival the effect of wood engraving.

The modern methods reproduce the black lines of a drawing direct. But the most practised engravers cut out the whites of a drawing with their graver from between the black lines. This undoubtedly allowed the artist a closer and less restricted use of line than modern illustration shows us. If the reader examines du Maurier's illustration for *The Adventures of Harry Richmond*, he will be able to see at a glance how, by cutting out the whites in the multiplicity of ivy leaves, detailed drawing has been re-interpreted in the engraving with great economy.

Some of the pleasantness of the effect of lines printed from a woodcut is due to the fact that they print a more clearly cut line. The line eaten in by "process" when examined under a very strong magnifying glass proves to be a slightly jagged one. But we should rejoice that the art of reproduction for journalistic purposes is free of the laborious method of engraving, and from the sort of work that was put up by over-tired engravers when they fought their last round to lose, against the modern invention of picture reproduction.

There is no rivalry in art. All the rivalry is in the business connected with it. A wood-engraving possesses a charm of its own for those whose sense of quality is delicate enough for its appreciation. The life of this art, apart from the purpose of weekly journalism, is safe. The life of any art is safe while it commands, as wood engraving does, the production of any particular effect in a way that cannot be rivalled.

According to Mr. Joseph Pennell, the first really important modern illustrated book in which wood was substituted for metal engraving appeared in France in 1830, and this authority asserts that in England, just before the invention of photographing on wood, some of the most marvellous engravings appeared that have ever been done in the country. "It is," he writes, "with the appearance of Frederick Sandys, Rossetti, Walker, Pinwell, A. Boyd, Houghton, Small, du Maurier, Keene, Crane, Leighton, Millais, and Tenniel, with the publication of the *Cornhill, Once a Week, Good Words, The Shilling Magazine*, and such books as Moxon's *Tennyson* that the best period of English illustration begins."

"The incessant output of illustration," he continues, "killed not only the artists themselves, but the process. In its stead arose a better, truer method, a more artistic method, which we are even now only developing."

But there is another side to this question. Illustration has lost something by the uniformity of style which the modern method encourages. Keene, whose style was supposed to suffer most at the hands of the engraver, found it more difficult than anyone to accommodate his free methods to the rules that govern the results of the modern process.

It may be noted that it was about the time of the transition from working on wood to work on paper that that slavery to the model began, which, as we have pointed out, has not in the end been without an unhappy effect in the loss of spontaneity to English Illustration.

As for the art of wood engraving itself, we hope it will now have a future like that which the arts of lithography and etching are enjoying. Reproduction by process serves commercial and journalistic purposes far better. The demands of commerce formed for this art, as it once formed for lithography, a chrysalis in which it perfected itself. Reproduction by process serves commercial purposes much better than ever wood-engraving could, but while the commercial demand for it lasted, as in the case of the arts of lithography and etching, it continued to improve; like them, let us hope, destined to find beautiful wings upon its release from the cramping demands of modern printing machines, in its practice by artists for sheer love of the peculiar qualities which are its own. It has been said that wood-engravers killed their own art so far as journalism was concerned by their surrender to commerciality with its frequent demand for the ready-to-hand rather than the superior thing. But his surrender was not the fault of the engravers, but was rendered inevitable by the advent of the middleman, to whom application was made by the Press for blocks, and whose employees all engravers were practically forced into becoming, instead of being able to retain their independence and make their own terms with the Press.

§ 7

In the British Museum some of the originals of du Maurier's *Punch* pictures may be seen. On the margins of these are the pencilled instructions of the Editor as to the scale of the reproduction, and very often pencil notes from Artist to Editor. This sort of thing—"If they have used my page for this week's number, telegraph to me as soon as you get this and I will have Social ready by 12 to-morrow (that is, if it be not too late for me.)" Or what is evidently an invitation to lunch—"Monday at 1 for light usual." The drawing where this particular note appears is of three little girls with their dolls. The legend in the artist's handwriting read as follows:—"*My papa's house has got a* conservatory! *My papa's house has got a* billiard-room! *My papa's house has got a* mortgage!!" This was printed with the much inferior legend: "Dolly taking her degrees (of comparison): '*My* doll's wood!' *My* doll's composition! '*My* doll's wax!'"

Some of these British Museum original drawings still retain in pencil the price du Maurier put upon them for sale. Of the period when the artist was drawing on a large scale with a view to reduction there is one of the "Things one would rather have expressed differently" series priced at twelve guineas. It gives an indication of the profits du Maurier sometimes was able to make from the original drawing. For the sake of comment on the low evening gown the half-dozen figures in this picture are all in back view. It is rather a dull twelve-guineas-worth. And this was evidently felt, as it remained unsold. The original of the very exquisite "Res angusta domi," the beautiful drawing of the nurse by the child's bed in the children's hospital, which appeared in *Punch*, vol. cviii. p. 102 (1894), is only priced at "Ten guineas."

Turning over the Museum drawings one often sees the liberties with the penknife by which the artist would secure difficult effects of snow, or of light on foliage. And sometimes in the margin there are pencil studies from which figures in the illustration have been re-drawn. And nearly always not altogether rubbed out is a first wording of the legend, repeated in ink in du Maurier's pretty "hand" beneath.

In turning over these drawings one finds him doing much more than merely suggesting pattern work in such things as wall-papers. There is one floral wall-paper in particular that we find him working out which will no doubt prove an invaluable reference another day as to the sort of decoration in which the subjects of Queen Victoria preferred to live, or were forced to by their tradesmen. Photographs of du Maurier's studio which appeared in a Magazine illustrating an interview with him at the time of the "Trilby" boom, reveal the squat china jars, the leaf fans, the upholstered "cosy corner" with its row of blue plates, with which all who know their *Punch* are familiar, and apparently the very wall-paper to which we have just referred. It certainly is the mark of a great artist to take practically whatever is before him for treatment. The artist with the genius for "interior" subjects seems to be able to re-interpret ugliness itself very often. Du Maurier's weak eyes prevented him from bearing the strain of outdoor work. He was practically driven indoors for his subjects; and in taking what was to hand—the very environment of the kind of people his drawings describe—he showed considerable genius. He succeeded in making whole volumes of *Punch* into a work of criticism on the domestic art of the nineteenth century.

ILLUSTRATION FOR "THE STORY OF A FEATHER" 1867.

Among the useful skits of du Maurier was that upon the conceited young man concealing appalling ignorance with the display of a still more appalling indifference to everything. The drawing among the Print-room series—"*It is always well to be well informed*"—is a good instance. It reveals a ballroom with couples dancing a quadrille. A lady asks her partner: "Who's my sister's partner, vis-à-vis, with the star and riband?" He: "Oh, he—aw—he's Sir Somebody Something, who went somewhere or othaw to look after some scientific fellow who was murdered, or something, by someone—!" The word *othaw* in this legend is itself pictorial. Du Maurier was like our own Max Beerbohm in this—his legends and drawings were inseparable. We find he has actually penned in the side margin of the drawing the words "othaw fellow," we suppose as a possible variant to "scientific fellow," and in the legend the word "other" has been written over with a thickened termination—"*aw.*" The usual first trial of the speech in pencil remains but partly obliterated by india-rubber at the top of the drawing.

In his series of "Happy Thoughts" du Maurier followed the course of the sort of rapid thought that precedes a tactful reply with real psychological skill. Take, for instance, his drawing of an artist sitting gloomily before his fire, caressed by his wife, who bends over him, saying, "You seem depressed, darling. Have you had a pleasant dinner?" Edwin: "Oh, pretty well; Bosse was in the chair, of course. He praised everybody's work this year except mine." Angelina: "Oh!

I'm so glad. *At last* he is beginning to look upon you as his rival and his *only* one." The wings of tact are sympathy. This drawing appeared in *Punch*, vol. xcvi. p. 222 (1889); it is signed with other drawings from 89 Porchester Terrace, April '89. Drawings in the Museum collection are signed from "Stanhope Terrace," "Hampstead," "Drumnadrochit," or apparently from wherever the artist happened to be when executing the work.

§8

Among our illustrations there is a portrait of Canon Ainger, representing the artist as a painter. Du Maurier's colour was never such that an injustice is done to it by reproducing it only by half-tone process. The interest of this portrait is in the psychological grasp of character it seems to show. The painter was in the habit of contributing interior *genre* scenes in water-colour to the Old Water-colour Society, of which he was made an Associate in 1881. That may be said against his painting, which may be said against the painting of so many eminent black-and-white men who have changed to the art of painting too late in the day. It shows failure to think in paint. An artist is only a great "black-and-white" artist because he thinks in that medium. Possibly, if there were no such thing as a "black-and-white" art, as we have it in journalism to-day, some of the greatest men in it would instead have been great painters. But successful transference to the one art after unusual mastery has been acquired in the other is rarely witnessed. To think in line, to see the world as resolving itself into the play of alternating lines, so to habituate thought and vision to that one aspect of everything is not the best preparation in the world for seeing it over again in another art where the element of line is not the chief incident of the impression to be created. Failure in the one art does not mean failure as an artist. Those artists who have worked in a variety of mediums with apparently equal success in each have always attained the ability to make each medium in turn express the same personal feeling. But nearly always there is in such cases that sacrifice of the inherent qualities of one or other of the mediums employed which a great virtuoso never makes.

Black-and-white men put themselves into an attitude of receptivity towards that aspect of things which suggests representation in line.

Their acquired sensitiveness in this respect is expressed in the learned character of their touch in drawing. Painters cultivate a similarly receptive attitude towards nature, but lay themselves open to receive a different impression of it. We might say of du Maurier that by the time he tried to apply himself to painting he had become constitutionally a black-and-white artist. Moreover, his impaired vision compromised the more complex range of effect represented in painting in a way that it never could the simplicity of good black-and-white work. How seriously threatened du Maurier's sight was at times we may know by the reliance he put upon being read to by others. Thus only did he manage to keep his small stock of visual energy in reserve for his artistic work.

§ 9

During the sixties and seventies the artist illustrated many works of fiction. The most notable instance was Thackeray's *Esmond* in 1868— a work which he had long wished to be chosen to illustrate.

Du Maurier had all his life an intense admiration for Thackeray. He inherited none of Thackeray's bitterness, but upon every other ground as an author, at least, he descends from Thackeray, notably in the studied colloquialism of his style when writing, and in a general friendliness to the Philistine. And in his drawings in *Punch* his satire is aimed in the same direction as Thackeray's always was. Like Thackeray, he was most at home on the plane where a social art, a delicate art of life is able to flourish. Of the concealed romanticist in du Maurier we have more than once already spoken. A Romanticist always turns to the past. Thackeray, in his lectures, also in the house he built for himself, and in a proposed but never finished history, went back into the past at least as far as Queen Anne's reign. *Esmond*, also of Queen Anne's reign, was the expression of a feature of Thackeray's temperament which never makes its full appearance in any other of his fictions. We believe that it was his own favourite among his works. But Thackeray did not succeed in expressing the whole of himself in the romantic vein; perhaps because he did not cultivate it from the start like Scott and Dumas. He was able to put more of himself into *Vanity Fair*. To think of Thackeray is to think first of *Vanity Fair*. From the unerring—because instinctive—

judgment of the world this book received recognition as his masterpiece.

Du Maurier had not so much of the genuine *flair* for the eighteenth century as Thackeray. At heart he was much more in sympathy with the pre-Raphaelites and the love of early romance, whatever his pretence to the contrary in his satire, *A Legend of Camelot*. But there was no illustrator of his time with a greater gift for the romantic novel of any period; and inevitably, he became, in due course, the illustrator of *Esmond*.

It is impossible to return to the past except by the path of poetry. It was possible to du Maurier in his illustrations to *Esmond*, because he was a poet. He used the effect of fading light in the sky seen through old leaded windows, and all the resources of poetic effect with a poet's and not an actor-manager's inspiration, wrapping the tale in the glamour in which Thackeray conceived it.

In 1865 du Maurier contributed a full page illustration and two vignettes to Foxe's *Book of Martyrs*, published in parts by Cassell. Other signed illustrations are by G.H. Thomas, John Gilbert, J.D. Watson, A.B. Houghton, W. Small, A. Parquier, R. Barnes, M.E. Edwards, and T. Morten. No book can be imagined which would afford the essential nature of his art less opportunity of showing itself than this one. He was no good at horrors, though his resourcefulness in the manifestation of emotional light and shadow was encouraged by the character of the full-page illustration which he had to supply. A signed full page appears in Part XVI., page 541. It is a scene in which the four martyrs, Bland, Frankesh, Sheterden, and Middleton, condemned by the Bishop of Dover, 25th June 1555, are shown being burned at the stakes. One of the martyrs certainly looks intensely smug with his hands folded as if he were at grace before a favourite dinner. Yes, du Maurier certainly failed to attain quite to the heights of the horror of this book.

The following year we have from the artist's pencil illustrations to a book of the heroine of which he was so fond that he named his own daughter after her. That book was Mrs. Gaskell's *Wives and Daughters*, "an everyday story," as it is called in its sub-title. For this story du Maurier's art was much more fitted than for any other. In it, certainly, and not in Foxe's book, we should expect his temperament to reveal itself—and we are not disappointed. It is here that du Maurier is at his best. His illustrations have a daintiness in this tale which they have nowhere else. A sign of the presence of fine art is the accommodation of style to theme. The illustrations had been made for this book when it appeared serially in the *Cornhill*, and were afterwards published in the issue in two volumes. There is a picture at the beginning of the second volume called "The Burning Gorse," in which du Maurier makes an imaginative appeal through landscape almost worthy of Keene.

ILLUSTRATION FOR "THE STORY OF A FEATHER" 1867.

The artist is again at his best in the work of illustrating fiction in the following year in Douglas Jerrold's *Story of a Feather*. It is the same refinement of technique that is evident as in Mrs. Gaskell's tale. One of du Maurier's greatest characteristics was charm. One is forced into ringing changes upon the word in the description of his work. But charm it is, more than ever, that characterises his illustrations to *The Story of a Feather*. The initial letters in this book afford him a succession of opportunities for displaying that inventive genius which is evident wherever he turns to the province of pure fancy. It was not for nothing apparently that he was the son of an inventor.

We have already spoken of his power in these days in the emotional use of light and shade. It is perhaps even in this light book—in the illustration reproduced opposite—that we have one of the best examples of this power. But this book is all through a gold-mine of the work of the real du Maurier.

Another work in which his art is to be found at this time is Shirley Brooks's *Sooner or Later* (1868). The novel does not seem treated with quite the same reverence and enthusiasm which has characterised his work in the books we have just described, but it is among the representative examples of his illustration in the sixties. This story also passed as a serial through *Cornhill*. In the same year, with E.H. Corbould, he provides illustrations to *The Book of Drawing-room Plays*, &c., a manual of indoor recreation by H. Dalton. It is not impossible that these were prepared long in advance of publication, for they are in a very much earlier manner than the illustrations we have been speaking of. In them du Maurier has not yet emerged from the influence of Leech—the first influence we encountered when a few years previously he joined himself to the band of those who solicit the publishers for illustrative work. From the point of view of our subject the book does not repay much study. In 1876, in illustrations to *Hurlock Chase, or Among the Sussex Ironworks*, by George E. Sargent, published by The Religious Tract Society, we have some pictures of extraordinary power, in which it is to be seen how much his contact with Millais and other great illustrators in the sixties inspired him, and developed his resources. His work has a "weight" in this book which was common to the best illustration of the period, a deliberation which shows the influence of Durer over the illustrators of the sixties, and also the influence of pre-Raphaelitism in precise elaboration of form. It is in lighter vein we find him again in the same year in Jemmett Browne's *Songs of Many Seasons*, published by Simpkin, Marshall & Co., and illustrated also by Walter Crane and others. Every now and then at this period du Maurier shows us a genius for "still-life" in interior *genre* which he did not seem to develop afterwards to the extent of the promise shown in these pictures. He gained at this time a very great deal in his art by the pre-Raphaelite influence. Never is he more exquisite than when he embraces detail. The need to produce with rapidity, and the effect of later fashions which did not suit his own nature so well, induced him to give up a very deliberate style suited to his quick perception of beauty in everyday incident, for one that sometimes only achieved emptiness in its attempt at breadth. But to have kept his pre-Raphaelite individuality with two such native impressionists as Keene and Whistler for his most intimate friends would have perhaps been more than could be expected of human nature. But it is true that he seemed to lose where those two artists proved they had everything to gain from a style that passed detail swiftly, treating it suggestively. They were by nature impressionable to a different aspect of life, and in self expression they required a different method.

Du Maurier's artistic creed that everything should be drawn from nature—and tables and chairs are "nature" for the artist—forced him to return again and again to accessible properties which could be fitted into his scenes. Notable among those were the big vases and the constantly reappearing ornamental gilt clock. Though drawn in black and white we are sure of its gilt, for it belongs to the Victorian period. It is to be met with in all the surviving drawing-rooms of the period—that is, it is to be met with in "Apartments."

Du Maurier next furnishes a frontispiece and vignettes, which we do not admire, to Clement Scott's *Round about the Islands* (1874).

In 1882 he is at work in the field he had made his own, illustrating the story of a fad that had always amused him, illustrating the craze he had helped to create, in *Prudence: A Story of Aesthetic London*, by Lucy C. Lillie. We hope the reader of this page does not think we should have read this book. We looked at the illustrations of a muscular curate—whom we took to be the hero—making an impressive entrance into a gathering of "æsthetes," and farther on leaving the church door with "Prudence"; we read the legend to the final illustration—"It was odd to see how completely Prudence forsook her brief period of æsthetic light"—and we came to our own conclusions. The illustrations are made very small in process of printing, but du Maurier's art never lost by reduction. A picture of a

Private View day in a Gallery—which at first makes one think of the Royal Academy, but in which the pictures are too well hung for that, and which is probably intended for the Grosvenor Gallery—is one of those admirable drawings of a fashionable crush with which du Maurier always excelled. In reviewing this book, however, we are already away from the most characteristic period of du Maurier's work as an illustrator of fiction. That was between 1860 and 1880. His line is altogether less intense in the next book we have to consider—Philips's *As in a Looking Glass* (1889). The falling off between this and the book we were reviewing here but a moment ago is the most evident feature of the work before us. We have, we feel, said good-bye to the du Maurier who added so much lustre to the illustrative work of the period just preceding its publication. But in *Punch* the vivacity of his art is still sustained; and long afterwards in *Trilby* he scores successes again. In later years du Maurier *allowed* in his originals for reduction, and the original cannot be rightly judged until the reduction is made. In the book under notice no reduction appears to have been made, and the drawings are consequently lacking in precision of detail. The book is a large drawing-room table book—in our opinion the most hateful kind of book that was ever made—occupying more space than any but the rarest works in the world are worth, giving more trouble to hold than it is possible for any but a great masterpiece to compensate for—and generally putting author and publisher in the debt of the reader, which is quite the wrong way round. The curious may see in this book what du Maurier's art was at its worst, and it may help them to estimate his achievement to note how even on this occasion it surpasses easily all later modern work in the same vein.

There is one other book, published in 1874, which du Maurier illustrated at that time which should be mentioned. It had, we believe, a great success of a popular kind. We refer to *Misunderstood*, by Florence Montgomery. In the light of the illustrations, which are in the artist's finest vein, one wonders how much of this success could with justice have been attributed to the illustrations. We are inclined to think not a little. These pictures show many of the most interesting qualities of his work. In the portrait of Sir Everard Duncombe, Misunderstood's father, we have a skill in portraying a type that cannot have failed in impressing readers with the reality of the character. The delicacy of du Maurier's psychology in this portrait of a middle-aged man of the period is in marked contrast with the improbability of so many of his renderings of elderly people wherever he went outside of his stock types. It justifies his realism and mistrust of memory drawing. Through his failure to sustain his interest in life always at this pitch his art at the end of his career showed just the lack of this close observation of character. It often then seems too content to rest its claims on accurate drawing, even when what was drawn was not worth accuracy. And this is the fault of all the modern school.

Good drawing does not so much interest us in things as in the drama centred in them. Thus we have actually such things as horror, passion, gentleness, and other invisible things conveyed to us in the lines of a drawing. We may indeed know genius from talent by the much more of the invisible which it transfers to visible line. Du Maurier, in drawing children, for instance, secures their prepossessing qualities. Drawing is great when it conveys something which in itself has not an outline—like the "atmosphere" of a Victorian drawing-room.

CAUTION
"DON'T KEEP YOUR BEER-BARREL IN THE SAME CELLAR AS
YOUR DUST-BIN!"
PUNCH, FEBRUARY 23, 1867.

§10

Intensely artistic natures make everything very self-expressive without conscious intention. For this reason an artist's handwriting tends to be more worth looking at than other people's. The draughtsman lavishes some of his skill upon his handwriting. This more particularly applies to the signature, which is written with fuller consciousness than other words. Artists, owing to their intense interest in "appearances," generally start by being a little self-conscious about their signature. But that period passes, and the autograph becomes set, to grow fragile with old age and shrink, but not to alter in its real characteristics. The signature at the foot of a picture presents a rather different problem from the signature at the foot of a letter. It must necessarily be a more deliberate and self-conscious affair, but it is no less expressive. German deliberation was never so well expressed as in Albert Durer's signature.

Self-advertisers always give themselves away with their signature. As a rule, the finer the artist the more natural his signature in style. And fine artists like to subscribe to the great tradition of their craft, that the work is everything, the workman only someone in the fair light of its effect; the name is added out of pride but not vain-glory, with that modest air with which a hero turns the conversation from himself. Naturalness and mastery arrive at the same moment; students cannot sign their works naturally. Du Maurier's signature passed through many transformations, and there were times, too, when the artist was quite undecided between the plentiful choice of his Christian names—George Louis Palmella Busson. An artist beginning his career at the present day with such a choice of names would most certainly have made use of the "Palmella" in full—an advertisement asset. But advertisement *is* vulgar. Du Maurier belonged to the Victorians, who were never vulgar.

FOOTNOTES:

[1] *The Life and Letters of Charles Samuel Keene*, by Charles Somes Layard. London: Sampson Low, Marston & Co., Ltd., 1892.

III

DU MAURIER AS AUTHOR

§1

Queen Victoria was the Queen of Hearts; her reign was the reign of sentiment. The redundancy of tender reference to Prince Albert at Windsor has been known to bore visitors to the town. Life must have been tiring in those days, tossed, as everyone was, if we believe the art of the time, from one wave of sentiment to another. Men went "into the city" to get a little rest, and there framed this code: that there should be no sentiment in business.

So the Victorians put their sentiment into art, into stories and illustrations. They put some of the best of their black-and-white art into a Magazine called *Good Words*. Only the Victorians could have invented such a title for a Magazine, or lived up to it.

The literary tradition of that time, so far as the novel was concerned, expired with du Maurier. He came near to having a style as natural as Thackeray's, and he was quite as sentimental.

Before he began to write novels, he prided himself upon the fact that a store of "plots" for novels lay undeveloped in his mind. It was the offer of a "plot" to Mr. Henry James one evening when they were walking up and down the High Street, Bayswater, that resulted in du Maurier becoming a novelist. Du Maurier told him the plot of *Trilby*. "But you ought to write that story," cried James. "I can't write," he replied; "I have never written. If you like the plot so much you may take it." Mr. James said that it was too valuable a present to take, and that du Maurier must write the story himself.

On reaching home that night he set to work. By the next morning he had written the first two numbers not of *Trilby* but of *Peter Ibbetson*. "It seemed all to flow from my pen, without effort in a full stream," he said, "but I thought it must be poor stuff, and I determined to look for an omen to learn whether any success would attend this new departure. So I walked out into the garden, and the very first thing that I saw was a large wheelbarrow, and that comforted me and reassured me, for, as you will remember, there is a wheelbarrow in the first chapter of *Peter Ibbetson*."[2]

Peter Ibbetson—"The young man, lonely, chivalrous and disquieted by a touch of genius," as the hero has been well described—was written for money, and brought its author a thousand pounds.

Peter Ibbetson was not put above *Trilby* in the author's lifetime; but we believe it to have much more vitality than the latter work. The actual writing of it was not perhaps taken quite so seriously as that of *Trilby*, and it gains nothing on that account; but it is a book in which there is intensity, in which everything is not spread out thinly as in *Trilby*. Du Maurier himself believed that *Peter Ibbetson* was the better book. It certainly witnesses to the nobility of the author's mind; it expresses the quick sympathy of the artist temperament— the instinct for finding extenuating circumstances which artists share with women, and which both rightly regard as the same thing as the sense of justice. The tale of *Peter Ibbetson* breathes a great human sympathy. The simplicity with which it is written adds to its effect. We cross a track of horror in it by the ray of a generous light. It is by this book I like to think that du Maurier will be remembered as a writer. It was characteristic of him that he could touch a theme that in all superficial aspects was sordid without the loss of the bloom of true romance. The real plot of this story, however, does not lie with incident, but with the maintenance of an elevated frame of mind in defiance of circumstances. The author realises that mind triumphs always more easily over matter than over "circumstances." To the damage of the plot he brings his hero the utmost psychic assistance from an inadmissible source, but the picture of the prisoner's soul prevailing in the face of complete temporal disaster is still a true one.

Du Maurier's publishers believed in *Trilby* from the very first. They began by offering double the *Peter Ibbetson* terms, while generously urging him to retain his rights in the book by accepting a little less in a lump sum and receiving a royalty. But so little faith did he pin to *Trilby* that he said "No!"

Within a few weeks the "boom" began. And when Harpers' saw what proportions it was likely to assume, they voluntarily destroyed the agreement, and arranged to allow him a handsome royalty on every copy sold. An admirer of Byron, du Maurier repudiated as cruelly unfair the poet's line, "Now Barabbas was a publisher." The publisher also handed over to him the dramatic rights with which he had parted for a small sum like fifty pounds, and thus he became a partner in the dramatic property called *Trilby* as a "play."

§ 2

Trilby was a name that had long lain *perdu* somewhere "at the back of du Maurier's head." He traced it to a story by Charles Nodier, in which Trilby was a man. The name Trilby also appears in a poem by Alfred de Musset. And to this name, and to the story of a woman which was once told to him, du Maurier's *Trilby* owed her birth. "From the moment the name occurred to me," he said, "I was struck with its value. I at once realised that it was a name of great importance. I think I must have felt as happy as Thackeray did when the title of *Vanity Fair* suggested itself to him."

Trilby is written with a daintiness that corresponds with the neatness of its illustrations. It has the attractiveness which du Maurier had such skill in giving. But though dealing with Bohemia, the author is conventional; that is, he keeps strictly to the surface of things. And every true sentiment of the book is spoilt by the quickly following laugh in which the author betrays his dread of being thought to take anything seriously.

BERKELEY SQUARE, 5 P.M.
PUNCH, AUGUST 24, 1867.

The machinery of the plot is crude; perhaps this reason as well as the delicate one assigned made Mr. Henry James refuse it. But du Maurier had a curious skill in revealing states of mind of real psychological and pathological interest. The sudden cessation of the power to feel affection, and of the ability to respond emotionally to nature, the curious loss of bloom in mental faculty in the case of Little Billee, in this we have an inquiry into a by no means unusual state of mind carried out with scientific exactness to an artistic end. Mr. Henry James would no doubt have preferred this phenomenon as the basis of a plot to the preposterous mesmerism which forms the plot of *Trilby*, he being one of the few who understand that a dramatic situation is a mental experience. In *Peter Ibbetson* the "dreaming truly"—the illusion that becomes as great as reality—is the phenomenon the author examines. "Dreaming truly" is like the ecstasy of the saints: it is the "will to believe" in the very act of willing.

Du Maurier was spoilt for romance by his long connection with a comic paper. It had become a habit with him to be on his guard against everything that could be travestied. This was the conventional side of du Maurier in evidence, as it is also in that other flaw in the simple story of *Trilby*—the adulation of worldly success. We find him constantly writing in this strain in the description of character: "He is now one of the greatest artists in the world, and Europeans cross the Atlantic to consult him"; or of another character: "And now that his name is a household word in two hemispheres"; and of another: "Whose pinnacle (of pure unadulterated fame) is now the highest of all," &c.

§3

In all his books the author shows some of that response to old-time associations which gives to authors like Dumas and Scott their freedom from things that only belong to the present moment—precisely the things, by the way, which do not last beyond the present. The consciousness that the experiences of life to be valued are the ones which unite us to those who preceded us in life, and which will in turn give us a share in the future, is in the possession of the Romantic school. But du Maurier seems to have felt himself paid to be funny, and to conceal his sense of romance as Jack Point concealed his love-sickness. His master, Thackeray, less than anyone apologised to his readers for the parade of his own feelings.

There is a note of smugness that spoils *Trilby*; in fact Little Billee, "frock-coated, shirt-collared within an inch of his life, duly scarfed and scarf-pinned, chimney-pot-hatted, most beautifully trousered, and balmorally booted," is the most insufferable picture of a hero of a romance. This person compromises the effect of the charmingly haunting presence of Trilby herself, and of the great-hearted gentleman in Taffy. There is, moreover, the failure to convince us of Little Billee's genius. We are not assisted to belief in the immortality of his works, by the illustrations of the mid-Victorian upholstery in the midst of which they were manufactured. On the other hand, we merely have a vision of the type of art which won popular success a generation ago, encouraged by the Royal Academy at the expense of something better, and keeping a large group of well-dressed painters so much in Society, that, like Little Billee himself, they actually grew tired of the great before the great had time to tire of them—"incredible as it may seem, and against nature."

Du Maurier put portraits of his friends into *Trilby*, softening the outlines, and giving the touches, legitimate in a work of art, which promote variation. He wrote impulsively, and a spirit of generous recognition of the achievements of all his friends almost ruined his book. The "lived happy ever afterwards" sentiment follows up every reference to them. In the famous character of "Joe Sibley" (Whistler)—afterwards altered to Antony, a Swiss, and ruined—a witty, a debonair and careless genius was created. Just such an impression was made upon us by this character as Whistler's own studied butterfly-pose in life seemed intended to make. It was with the greatest regret we missed the fascinating figure from the novel when published in book form, a regret even confessed to by Whistler himself, though he had not been able to refrain from dashing into print over its publication. There was none other of the Bohemians described that so endeared himself to us, or that was so alive— witnessing to the degree to which Whistler's personality affected those with whom he was thrown in contact. Du Maurier represented a character in Sibley with the defects of his qualities, to the greater emphasis of the qualities. To attribute to a man the genius to be king of Bohemia, and to receive from everyone forgiveness for everything, *à cause de ses gentillesses* to make him witty also, and a most exquisite and original artist—this would have been enough for most men, though it was not enough for Whistler. Joe Sibley, not Little Billee, is the real creation of "an artist" that is in the book.

ILLUSTRATION FOR "ESMOND"

§ 4

When *Trilby* was put on the English stage a girl to play the heroine's part had to be found. That was the first problem. And speaking of the fact that a *Trilby* did appear almost immediately, du Maurier said, "There is a school which believes that wherever Art leads

Nature is bound to follow. I ought to belong to it, if there is." A *Trilby* was heard of; more, du Maurier had often commented upon the beauty of the lady when she was a child living near him at Hampstead Heath. He inquired her name. She was already on the stage, and showing promise as an actress. He still felt sceptical, we are told, and so a photograph was sent. He said, "No acting will be wanted; for here is Trilby." Miss Baird was interviewed. "In face and manner," said du Maurier, telling the story of the interview, "she seemed still more Trilby-like than ever; but Mr. Tree, who was present, was on thoughts of acting-power intent. And when he gravely announced that to be an actress a woman should not be well-born and well-bred, and that if possible she should have had her home in the wings or the gutter, I considered the matter settled. We drove away in silence, and I, at any rate, in gloom. For Miss Baird, refined and gentle, and well-born and well-bred, was still Trilby for me, and I flatly refused to see either of the ladies whom Mr. Tree had in mind. Finally, he thought he would see Miss Baird again, and with her read over a scene or two. He got another cab—returned there and then—in forty-eight hours the engagement was made."

It may be found interesting if we revive here a criticism which throws light on the first reception of the adaption of *Trilby* for the stage. The play was put on before the *Trilby* boom had spent itself, but critics would, from the nature of their species, be rather prejudiced against, than carried away in favour of, anything which came in with a "boom" that was not of their own making. There was a criticism written of the play at the time by Mr. Justin Huntly Macarthy which, quoted, will give us the history of the "boom." It was his good fortune to be in the United States "when," he says, "the taste for *Trilby* became a passion, when the passion grew into a mania and the mania deepened into a madness," and he noted that in England the play and not the novel kindled the passion; though in the criticism of the novel, classed as it had been even in this country with the work of Thackeray, he could only recall one note of dispraise, "so earnest and scornful that, in its loneliness, it seemed to fall like the clatter of a steel glove in a house of prayer." He recalled a friend of his goaded to ferocity by another's exuberance of rapture for some latter-day singers, crying out "Hang your Decadents! Humpty-Dumpty is worth all they ever wrote." "This," he continued, "is a variety of the mood which accepts *Trilby*. In *Trilby* we get back, as it were, to Humpty-Dumpty—to its simplicity at least, if not to its pitch of art. The strong man and the odd man and the boy man, brothers in Bohemianism, brothers in art, brothers in love for youth and beauty; the girl, the fair, the kind, the for-ever-desirable, pure in impurity, and sacred even in shame; the dingy evil genius who gibbers in Yiddish to the God he denies; the hopeless, devoted musician, whose spirit in a previous existence answered to the name of Bowes; the mother who makes the appeal that so many parents have made on behalf of their sons to fair sinners since the days when Duval the elder interviewed Marguerite Gauthier; all this company of puppets please in their familiarity, their straightforwardness, their undefeated obviousness, very much as a game of bowls on a village green with decent rustics, or a game of romps in a rose-garden with laughing children, might please after a supper with Nana or an evening with the Theosophists."

This seems to us to diagnose the case as far as the success of the play was concerned. But as regards the book at which it was partly aimed, it is wide of the mark. There is something in a work of fiction when it is of sufficient power to make a success simply as fiction which cannot be carried over the footlights. If we only knew Shakespeare through seeing him acted we should rate him much lower than we do. The success of Shakespeare upon the stage rests with certain qualities that can only properly tell upon the stage. But great as these qualities are, in Shakespeare's case they far from represent his whole art; there remains unexpressed the fragrance of field and flower, the secrets of mood, which do not lie with facts that acting can express, and which float like a perfume between us and the pages. All this the dust of stage carpentry destroys, and the unnaturalness of lime-light dispels. The charm in *Trilby* is overlaid by the obvious, but the charm is there for the reader, just as the obviousness is there for the stage when the charm is gone in the adaptation. The stage is the throne of the obvious. It is possible for art to be obvious and great, as the art of Turner was in painting. His art was theatrical. It is the obvious that is theatrical. For that which is theatrical, as the word implies, must be spectacular. Theatricality before everything else in this world, in any art, achieves wide and popular success, the kind of success that

Turner achieves in the pictures for which the English public admire him.

Mr. W.D. Howells, in an article written just after the novelist's death, said:[3] —"It was my good fortune to have the courage to write to du Maurier when *Trilby* was only half printed, and to tell him how much I liked the gay sad story. In every way it was well that I did not wait for the end, for the last third of it seemed to me so altogether forced in its conclusions that I could not have offered my praises with a whole heart, nor he accept them with any pleasure, if the disgust with its preposterous popularity, which he so frankly, so humorously expressed, had then begun in him."

UNPUBLISHED DRAWING FROM SKETCH-BOOK

The American critic describes the fact of du Maurier commencing novelist at sixty and succeeding, as one of the most extraordinary things in the history of literature, and without parallel. Perhaps the parallel has been shown in the case of Mr. de Morgan. Mr. Howells also speaks of du Maurier perfecting an attitude recognisable in Fielding, Sterne, Heine, and Thackeray—the confidential one. Du Maurier's *Trilby* was a confidence. But he adds, "It wants the last respect for the reader's intelligence—it wants whatever is the very greatest thing in the very greatest novelists—the thing that convinces in Hawthorne, George Eliot, Tourgénief, Tolstoy. But short of this supreme truth, it has every grace, every beauty, every charm." The word "Every" here seems to us an American exaggeration. We should ask ourselves whether in spite of all its confidentialness *Trilby* makes an intimate revelation. The rare quality of intimacy, that is the greatest thing in the very greatest novels.

The "boom" of *Trilby*, we are told, surprised du Maurier immensely, for he had not taken himself *au sérieux* as a novelist. Indeed it rather distressed him when he reflected that Thackeray never had a "boom."

§5

Although du Maurier had said that his head was full of plots the supply seemed to have run thin by the time he set to work on *The Martian*. The value of this book rests with its autobiographical character. The knot is not tied in the first half and unravelled in the second, after the approved manner in which plots should be woven. The story is chiefly a record of people and places, vivid, and written in a breathless, chatty style. It somewhat resembles the conversation of a boy on returning from his holidays. It reveals a perfectly amazing resource in imparting life to mere description. As a writer, du Maurier seemed immediately to acquire a style unlike that of anyone else. Everything is described with a zest that carries the reader along, and this manner is even extended to things that are not worth describing. But he was always slightly apologetic with pen in hand, never permitting himself the professional air, or giving a full challenge to criticism by disclaiming the privileges of a distinguished amateur.

ILLUSTRATION FOR "THE ADVENTURES OF HARRY
RICHMOND"
THE CORNHILL, 1870.

In *Peter Ibbetson* the artist told the story of his childhood; in *Trilby* he recounted the brightest period of his Bohemian youth; in *The Martian* he records the nature of the shock he received from threatened blindness, and the depression of days before his genius had discovered itself and revealed the prospect of a great career to him. The effect of Pentonville, the grey suburb, and of the absence of worthy companions upon a romantic, highly-strung young man in *Peter Ibbetson* is quite autobiographical, as is the description of student life in Paris by which afterwards the uninspiring environment is replaced. The continuation of the studentship at Antwerp, the consultation with the specialist at Dusseldorf, completes the story of du Maurier's life until he came to London. There is literally nothing that a biographer could add to it. And du Maurier wrote his autobiography thus, in tales, which are histories too, in their graphic description of the aspect of places and people at a given time. Up to the day when the artist came to London to seek employment from the publishers he seems to have had disheartening times. In the last years of his life, when he went over the ground of these early experiences in his books, it was, as is evident from the style, in the mood of one who had survived danger by flood and field to recount his tales in an atmosphere of peace he had hardly hoped to realise.

It is evident from his books that he had many inward experiences of a dramatic kind; that his life was only uneventful upon the surface, and in appearance. In each of his novels, as we have seen, the rather crude machinery of his plot secures the revelation of a curious, but a not at all uncommon state of mind. He experimented empirically in psychology, interesting himself in the processes of his own mind. No one can doubt that in more than in outward incident his novels were autobiographical; that also he drew upon the resources of his personal history for some of the less usual and partly religious frames of mind in which his "Heroes," each in his own way, outwit the apparently ugly intentions of destiny towards themselves.

§ 6

Du Maurier's literary contributions to *Punch* were bound up in the volume *A Legend of Camelot, &c.*, issued from the *Punch* office in 1898. Besides the title-piece, a satire of some length upon the mediævalism of the pre-Raphaelites, the book contains shorter pieces—"Flirts in Hades," "Poor Pussy's Nightmare," "The Fool's Paradise, or Love and Life," "A Lost Illusion," "Vers Nonsensiques," "L'Onglay à

Parry," "Two Thrones," "A Love-Agony," "A Simple Story," "A Ballad of Blunders" (after Swinburne's "Ballad of Burdens"), and then a story in prose, "The Rise and Fall of the Jack Spratts: A tale of Modern Art and Fashion." All the poetry is in the ballad strain, and by its monotony the reader is put into the right condition to receive a shock from some felicitous twist at the end of a line. Thus it is almost impossible to quote from them. The humour rests in each case with the whole of the skit; and in the case of one of the best of the whole series, "A Love-Agony," a poem for a picture by Maudle, given, there must be understanding on the reader's part, of the art "cult" against which it is directed.

"The Rise and Fall of the Jack Spratts" is du Maurier's first attempt at a work of fiction. It is significant that in style it has the lightness of touch that would be expected from the disciple of Thackeray, and that afterwards won by its "taking" character the hearts of the readers of *Trilby*. It is the story of a painter, his wife and their twin children. It opens with a picture of them at home, Jack Spratt dreaming, even in those days, of Post-Impressionism, showing that du Maurier was a prophet, "dreaming of the ante-pre-Raphaelite school. In the depths of his bliss a feeling of discouragement would steal over him as he thought of those immortal works, showing thereby that he was a true artist, ever striving after the light. He little dreamt in his modesty that, young and inexperienced though he might be, his pictures were even quainter than theirs; for not only could he already draw, colour, compose, and put into perspective quite as badly as they did, but he had over them the advantage of a real lay figure to copy, whereas they had to content themselves with the living model."

"The amusements of this happy pair were the simplest, healthiest, and most delightful kind; they never went to the play, nor to balls or dances, which they thought immodest—(indeed they were not even asked)—nor read such things as novels, magazines, or the newspaper; nor visited exhibitions of modern art, which they held in contempt, as they did all things modern; ... and they were devoted to music, not that of the present day, which they despised, nor that of the future, of which they had never heard; nor English music, which was not old enough." Of their friends, "They were few, but true and trusty, with remarkably fine heads for a painter ... their deportment grave, sad and very strange; for the death of the early Italian masters still weighed on their soul with all the force of some recent domestic bereavement. They looked on themselves and each other and the Jack Spratts, and were looked upon by the Jack Spratts in return as the sole incarnation on this degenerate earth of all such as had still managed to survive there; and so they were always telling each other and everyone else they met. And no wonder, for they were marvellously accomplished; being each of them painter, sculptor, architect, poet, critic and engraver, all in one; and all this without ever having learnt...."

"In their hours of sickness alone the Spratts were as other people, and sent immediately for the nearest medical practitioner (or leech, as they preferred to call him); their only sickness to speak of had arisen from once feasting mediaevally on an old roast peacock, in company with the trusty friends, who had also been taken very bad on that occasion; and they ever afterwards avoided that dish, but at their banquets would have the peacock's head and what was left of its tail tacked on to some more digestible bird...."

"As staunch Radicals, they hated the aristocracy, whose very existence they ignored; shunned the professional class, which they scorned, on account of its scientific and utilitarian tendency; and loathed the middle class, from which they had sprung, because it was Philistine; and although they professed to deeply honour the working man, they very wisely managed to see as little of him as they possibly could."

Owing to the sudden success of a picture—which scandalised his trusty friends—and the beauty of his wife, the model for the picture, Jack woke up one morning and found himself famous. They were lionised. Mrs. Spratt's deep-rooted dislike to the female dress of the present day did not last much longer than her life-long prejudice against the aristocracy; she discarded the mediæval garments she had hitherto worn with such disdain for the eccentricities of modern fashion, and put herself into the hands of the best dressmaker in town. And thus snubbing, and being snubbed, dressing and dancing and feasting and flirting, did she soar higher and higher in her butterfly career. The denouement comes when they are cut out by "Ye rising Minnows"—an American sculptor—one Pygmalion F. Minnow—whose wife was twice as beautiful as Mrs. Spratt.

Another shorter prose skit of du Maurier's which is included in the same book satirises the splendid sort of hero, who conceals beneath a mask of indifference the power to do anything on earth better than anybody else.

These prose skits show the neat irony that *Punch* was willing to encourage by attaching du Maurier to the literary, as well as to the artistic, staff. But we think it may be said that du Maurier hadn't the heart to go on with a class of writing in which his great tendency to sentimentalise would have been out of place.

§ 7

In 1890 du Maurier contributed two papers to the *Art Journal* entitled "The Illustrating of Books from the Serious Artist's Point of View." It was an attempt to write down the ideas that had controlled him in book illustration. The artist begins the article by protesting that of all subjects in the world it is the one upon which he has the least and fewest ideas, and that such ideas as he has consist principally of his admiration for illustrations by others. He separates readers into two classes—those who visualise what they read with the mind's eye so satisfactorily that they want the help of no pictures, and those—the greater number, he thinks—who do not possess this gift, to whom to have the author's conceptions embodied for them in a concrete form is a boon. The little figures in the picture are a mild substitute for the actors at the footlights. The arrested gesture, the expression of face, the character and costume, may be as true to nature and life as the best actor can make them. His test of a good illustrator is that the illustrations continue to haunt the memory when the letterpress is forgotten. He cites Menzel as the highest example of such performance. He next refers to the illustrated volume of Poems by Tennyson in 1860, for which Millais and Rossetti and others designed small woodcuts, the publishing of which, he says, made an epoch in English book illustration, importing a new element to which he finds it difficult to give a name. "I still adore," he says, "the lovely, wild, irresponsible moon-face of Oriana, with a gigantic mailed archer kneeling at her feet in the yew-wood, and stringing his fatal bow; the strange beautiful figure of the Lady of Shalott, when the curse comes over her, and her splendid hair is floating wide, like the magic web; the warm embrace of Amy and her cousin (when their spirits rushed together at the touching of the lips), and the dear little symmetrical wavelets beyond; the queen sucking the poison out of her husband's arm; the exquisite bride at the end of the Talking Oak; the sweet little picture of Emma Morland and Edward Grey, so natural and so modern, with the trousers treated in quite the proper spirit; the chaste Sir Galahad, slaking his thirst with holy water, amid all the mystic surroundings; and the delightfully incomprehensible pictures to the Palace of Art, that gave one a weird sense of comfort, like the word 'Mesopotamia,' without one's knowing why."

In the second paper he makes interesting reflections on Thackeray and Dickens. "When the honour devolved upon me of illustrating *Esmond*," he writes, "what would I not have given to possess sketches, however slight, of Thackeray's own from which to inspire myself—since he was no longer alive to consult. For although he does not, any more than Dickens, very minutely describe the outer aspect of his people, he visualised them very accurately, as these sketches prove."

"I doubt if Dickens did, especially his women—his pretty women— Mrs. Dombey, Florence, Dora, Agnes, Ruth Pinch, Kate Nickleby, little Emily—we know them all through Hablot Browne alone—and none of them present any very marked physical characteristics. They are sweet and graceful, neither tall nor short; they have a pretty droop in their shoulders, and are very ladylike; sometimes they wear ringlets, sometimes not, and each would do very easily for the other."

In 1868 Messrs. Harper published in book form under the title *Social Pictorial Satire* a series of articles which du Maurier had written in *Harper's Magazine*, and which had originally formed the substance of lectures which he had delivered in the prominent towns of England. He speaks first of his great admiration of Leech in his youth. "To be an apparently hopeless invalid at Christmas-time in some dreary, deserted, dismal little Flemish town, and to receive *Punch's Almanac* (for 1858, let us say) from some good-natured friend in England— that is a thing not to be forgotten! I little dreamed that I should come to London again, and meet John Leech and become his friend; that I should be, alas! the last man to shake hands with him before his death (as I believe I was), and find myself among the officially invited mourners by his grave; and, finally, that I should inherit, and fill for so many years (however indifferently), that half-page in *Punch* opposite the political cartoon, and which I had loved so well when he was the artist!" Du Maurier draws a pleasant portrait of his friend, sympathetically, and very picturesquely analyses his art, which has, he says, the quality of inevitableness. Of "Words set to Pictures" his long description of Leech's pretty woman is as good as anything that can be read of the kind. Then he sketches the characteristics of Charles Keene's personality and passes on to his art:—"From the pencil of this most lovable man, with his unrivalled power of expressing all he saw and thought, I cannot recall many lovable characters of either sex or of any age."

ILLUSTRATION FOR "THE ADVENTURES OF HARRY RICHMOND"
THE CORNHILL, 1871.

But the tribute to the craftsmanship, the skill, the ease and beauty of Keene's line, to his knowledge of effect, to the very great artist is unmeasured. In fulfilment of his contract du Maurier speaks of himself and his "little bit of paper, a steel pen, and a bottle of ink— and, alas! fingers and an eye less skilled than they would have been if I had gone straight to a school of art instead of a laboratory for chemistry!" He says very little about himself. He concludes with a review of social pictorial satire considered as a fine art. It is evident from the lecture that du Maurier was an illustrator by instinct as well as training. "Now conceive," says he, speaking of Thackeray, "that the marvellous gift of expression that he was to possess in words had been changed by some fairy at his birth into an equal gift of expression by means of the pencil, and that he had cultivated the gift as assiduously as he cultivated the other, and, finally, that he had exercised it as seriously through life, bestowing on innumerable little pictures in black and white all the art and wisdom, the wide culture, the deep knowledge of the world and of the human heart, all the satire, the tenderness, the drollery, and last, but not least, that incomparable perfection of style that we find in all or most that he has written—what a pictorial record that would be!"

"The career of the future social pictorial satirist is," he continues, "full of splendid possibilities undreamed of yet.... The number of youths who can draw beautifully is quite appalling. All we want for my little dream to be realised is that, among these precocious wielders of the pencil, there should arise here a Dickens, there a Thackeray, there a George Eliot or an Anthony Trollope...."

Does not this precisely sum the situation up? Du Maurier could not live to foresee that, for all the expert skill of modern illustration, the "youths who can draw beautifully" lack "a point of view." It was the possession of this that distinguished Thackeray, George Eliot, Trollope, Leech, and du Maurier.

FOOTNOTES:

[2] The circumstances in which du Maurier took up novel-writing, and the history of the staging of *Trilby* in England were related by

him to Mr. R.H. Sherard for an "Interview" which appeared in *McClure's Magazine* 1895. And I have referred to this source for the genealogy of the artist, as given by himself, and particulars of his early life.—AUTHOR.

[3] *English Society*, "Du Maurier." London: Osgood, McIlvaine and Co. Introduction: W.D. Howells.

IV

LIFE OF THE ARTIST

§1

To write of the work of an artist who is not a contemporary without reference to the circumstances of his life would be an incomplete performance, and yet criticism and biography are hardly ever happily fused. The gifts of a biographer are of a kind very dissimilar to those employed in criticism. The true biographer loves uncritically every detail that has to do with his subject, as a portrait-painter loves every detail that has to do with the appearance of his sitter. The best portraits, whether in biography—which is nothing if it is not portraiture—or in painting, are those in which the interpreter has been in a wholly receptive mood. This is not the critical attitude, which involuntarily takes arms against first one thing and then another in the subject before it; and this sensitiveness is in proportion to the critic's interest in his subject.

Du Maurier told us the story of himself completely in his novels. It was said of de Quincey that in his writings he could tell the story of his own life and no other. This might be said of du Maurier too.

The story of his childhood, as we read it through his books, gives us the picture of an extremely sensitive and romantic child possessed of a great power of responding affectionately to the scenes in which he grew up, as well as to the people who surrounded him. It is this sentiment for place as well as for people that sometimes gives us in his books a remarkable poetic strain—a strain like music in its caressing revival of old associations. And we really get a very accurate idea of the inward story of the artist when we contrast this temperamental sensitiveness with the kind of work upon which he employed his skill during the chief part of his career.

Everywhere in du Maurier's life we find the testimony to his sweetness of disposition. He had the great loyalty to friends which is really loyalty to the world at large, made up of possible friends.

Friends are not an accident, but they are made by a process of natural selection, which, if we are wise and generous, we do not attempt to superintend.

PROXY

"AS YOU'RE GOING TO SAY YOUR PRAYERS, MAUD, PLEASE MENTION I'M SO DREADFULLY TIRED I CAN'T SAY MINE TO-NIGHT, BUT I'LL BE SURE TO REMEMBER TO-MORROW!"

PUNCH'S ALMANACK, 1874.

Du Maurier was optimistic, he had the genius for keeping tragedy at bay; for enduring, for instance, such a dark cloud constantly threatening as blindness without claiming pity. It is easy for such people to impart charm in whatever art they practise. And it is not true, as modern novelists and playwrights seem to imagine, that "depth" always implies what is sinister, and that only the surface of life is charming. Let us once again believe in fragrance in art. Summer is as great as winter. Within a sweet-smelling blossom is the whole profound history of a tree struggling to survive the vengeance of frost and gales. It is the fragrant things of life that contain all that has been conserved through unkind weather.

One of the chief influences in du Maurier's life was his admiration of Thackeray. This revealed sympathy with greatness. Thackeray was one who was greater in life than in his art, as are all the greatest artists. He was great as a man of the world. In a short life his presence made itself prevail everywhere in London. It requires, too, considerable genius to live only in precisely the street and the house in London you want to. This Thackeray managed to do; and to know only the people you want to, as Thackeray did. This is real sovereignty.

There was a reserve about du Maurier in manner when he encountered complete strangers. He retained the detached and distant manner with slight acquaintances which his role of an observer in Society had taught him. Like all those who have an exceptionally loyal friendship to give, he could not pretend to give it to every person introduced to him. In this he was, of course, no true Bohemian. In Bohemian circles it is the fashion to make extravagant use of terms of endearment and to fall upon the neck at first meetings, and men like du Maurier reserve the display of affection for the home.

Art-critics and secretaries of Art Galleries, frame-makers and all those whose business throws them into constant contact with living artists and their art, know how exactly like their pictures artists always are, their work being immediately expressive of their own fibre, coarse or refined. Du Maurier's art reveals a marked preference for certain kinds of people. In life too he was selective; knowing well whom he liked, and in whom he wished to inspire regard.

The artist's family was of the small nobility of France. The name Palmella was given him in remembrance of the great friendship between his father's sister and the Duchess de Palmella, who was the wife of the Portuguese Ambassador to France. The real family name was Busson; the "du Maurier" came from the Château le Maurier, built in the fifteenth century, and still standing in Anjou or Maine. It belonged to du Maurier's cousins, the Auberys, and in the seventeenth century it was the Auberys who wore the title of du Maurier; and an Aubery du Maurier, who distinguished himself in that century, was Louis of that name, French Ambassador to Holland. The Auberys and the Bussons married and intermarried, the Bussons assuming the territorial name of du Maurier.

George du Maurier's grandfather's name was Robert Mathurin Busson du Maurier, *Gentilhomme verrier*—gentleman glass-blower. Until the Revolution glass-blowing was a monopoly of the *gentilshommes*, no commoner might engage in the industry, at that time considered an art. The Busson genealogy dates from the twelfth century. The novelist made use of many of the names which occur in papers relating to his family history, in *Peter Ibbetson*.

Du Maurier's father was a small *rentier*, deriving his income from the family glass-works in Anjou. He was born in England, whither the artist's grandfather had fled to escape the Revolution and the guillotine, returning to France in 1816.

His grandmother was a bourgeoise, by name Bruaire, a descendant of Jean Bart, the admiral. His grandfather was not rich, and while in England mainly depended on the liberality of the British Government, which allowed him a pension of twenty pounds a year for each member of his family. He died a schoolmaster at Tours.

The mother of the artist was an Englishwoman married to his father at the British Embassy in Paris, and the artist was born in Paris on March 6, 1834, in a little house in the Champs Elysées. His parents removed to Belgium in 1863, where they stayed three years. When the child was five they came to London, taking 1 Devonshire Terrace, Marylebone Road—the house which had been formerly occupied by Charles Dickens. Du Maurier remembered riding in the park, on a little pony, escorted by a groom, who led his pony by a strap. One day there cantered past a young woman surrounded by horsemen; at the bidding of his groom he waved his hat, and the lady smiled and kissed her hand to him. It was Queen Victoria with her equerries.

The father grew very poor. He was a man of scientific tastes, and lost his money in inventions which never came to anything. After a year in Devonshire Terrace the family had to wander again, going to Boulogne, where they lived at the top of the Grand Rue. Here the artist said they lived in a beautiful house, and had sunny hours and were happy.

Apropos of du Maurier's early homes, Sir Francis Burnand, in his *Records and Reminiscences*, tells an amusing story, which, whilst of necessity abbreviating, we shall try to give as nearly as possible in his own words. Some members of the *Punch* staff who, with the proprietors, were visiting Paris during the Exhibition year of 1889, took a drive in the neighbourhood of Passy. Du Maurier, who had not stayed in Paris for some years, pointed out house after house as being his birthplace. He started with the selection of a small but attractive suburban residence, afterwards correcting himself and pointing to a house much more attractive-looking than the first. Soon, however, the puzzled expression which his companions had noticed in him before, returned to his face, and he called a halt for the third time, pointing to a large house in an extensive garden with a fountain. "No," he exclaimed with conviction, "I was wrong. This is where I was born. There's the fountain, there are the green shutters! and in *that* room!" The party descended again and poured out libations. After the sleepy stage of a long drive had been reached, du Maurier awoke, and, as if soliloquising, muttered, "No, no, I was wrong, absurdly wrong. But I see my mistake." And he aroused his companions to view a fine mansion approached by a drive.

"Yes," he exclaimed, "the other places were mistakes. It is so difficult to remember the exact spot where one was born. But there can be no doubt about this. *Cocher! Arrêtez! s'il vous plaît*," he cried, and he was about to open the door and descend, when William Bradbury, of the party, stopped him.

"No, you don't, Kiki; you've been born in three or four places already, and we've drunk your health in every one of 'em; so we won't do it again till you've quite made up your mind where you *were* born."

In vain du Maurier protested. "You bring us out for a holiday, you take us about everywhere, and you won't let a chap be born where he likes." But Mr. Bradbury was inexorable; the door was closed, the coachman grinned, cracked his whip, and away they went, the party siding with Mr. Bradbury in objecting to pulling up at every inn to toast the occasion.

Sir Francis speaks of what fun du Maurier was at such times, and of never remembering having seen him so boyish, so "Trilbyish" as on the occasion of the memorable visit.

From Boulogne du Maurier was brought by his family to Paris, to live in an apartment on the first floor of the house No. 80 in the Champs Elysées. In the artist's manhood the ground and first floor were a café, and he said he felt sorry to look up at the windows from which his mother used to watch his return from school, and see waiters bustling about and his home invaded.

§ 2

He went to school at the age of thirteen, in the Pension Froussard, in the Avenue du Bois de Boulogne. He remembered with affection his master Froussard, who became a deputy after the Revolution of 1848. He owned to being lazy, with no particular bent; but he worked really hard, he confessed, for one year. He made a number of friends, but of his comrades at that school only one distinguished himself in after life, Louis Becque de Fouquière, the writer, whose life has been written by M. Anatole France.

The artist went up for his *bachot*, his baccalaureate degree, at the Sorbonne, and was plucked for his written Latin version. It vexed him and his mother, for they were poor at the time, and it was important that he should do well. His father was then in England. Du Maurier crossed to him before informing him of his failure, miserable with the communication he had to make. They met at the landing at London Bridge, and at the sight of his utterly woebegone face, guessing the truth, his father burst into a roar of laughter, which, said the son afterwards, gave him the greatest pleasure he ever experienced.

His father was scientific, and hated everything that was not science. Du Maurier, with his enthusiasm for Byron, had to meet this attitude as best he could. His father never reproached him for the failure in the *bachot* examination. He had made up his mind that his son was intended for a scientist, and determined to make him one, putting him as a pupil at the Birkbeck Chemical Laboratory of University College, where he studied chemistry under Dr. Williamson. The son's own ambition at that time was to go in for music and singing. "My father," he said, "possessed the sweetest, most beautiful voice that I have ever heard; and if he had taken up singing as a profession, would most certainly have been the greatest singer of his time. In his youth he had studied music at the Paris Conservatoire, but his family objected to his following the profession, for they were Legitimists and strong Catholics, and held the stage in that contempt that was usual at the beginning of the last century."

The artist himself as a youth was crazy about music, and used to practise his voice wherever and whenever he could. But his father discouraged him. The father died in his arms, singing one of Count de Ségur's songs.

QUEEN PRIMA-DONNA AT HOME

CHORUS. "O, MAMMA!—DEAR MAMMA!—DARLING
MAMMA!! DO LEAVE
OFF!!!"

(SHOWING THAT NO ONE IS A PROPHET IN HIS OWN
COUNTRY.)

PUNCH, NOVEMBER 7, 1874.

He remained at the Birkbeck Laboratory for two years, leaving there in 1854, when his parent, still convinced of the future before his son in the pursuit of science, set him up on his own account in a chemical laboratory in Barge Yard, Bucklersbury, in the City. The house is still standing. "It was," says du Maurier, "a fine laboratory, for my father, being a poor man, naturally fitted it up in the most expensive style." "The only occasion," he continues, "on which the sage of Barge Yard was able to render any real service to humanity was when he was engaged by the directors of a Company for working certain gold mines in Devonshire which were being greatly boomed, and to which the public was subscribing heavily, to go down to Devonshire to assay the ore. I fancy they expected me to send them a report likely to further tempt the public. If this was their expectation, they were mistaken, for after a few experiments I went back to town and told them that there was not a vestige of gold in the ore. The directors were of course very dissatisfied with this statement, and insisted on my returning to Devonshire to make further investigation. I went and had a good time of it down in the country, for the miners were very jolly fellows; but I was unable to satisfy my employers, and sent up a report which showed the public that the whole thing was a swindle, and so saved a good many people from loss."

Du Maurier told the story of this business in *Once a Week* in 1861; it is written in a highly amusing strain.

We have taken relevant extracts, as follows, from the amusing story, partly because it exhibits the artist for the first time as an Author, and partly because it continues the narrative of his life:—

§ 3

"Somebody who took a great interest in me (my father) had just established me in the City as an analytical chemist and mining engineer. Now, if there was one thing in the world for which I was peculiarly, and I may even say extraordinarily, unfit, it was that very useful profession; but it is a well-known fact that the fondest parents are not always the most discriminating in the choice of professions for their sons. So I had spent two years in a school of chemistry, attending lectures and performing analyses, qualitative and quantitative, and various other chemical experiments, which I used to think very droll and amusing, in order to fit myself for my future career, and at length, thanks to my father's kindness, I found myself master of a laboratory which had been arranged in a manner regardless of expense, with water and gas laid on in every possible corner, and bottles, chemical stoves, and scales, &c., of a most ornamental brightness and perfection.

"Here I waited for employment daily, and entertained my friends with sumptuous hospitality at lunch and supper; here also I occasionally astonished my mother and sister by dexterously turning yellow liquids into blue ones, and performing other marvels of science—accomplishments which I have almost entirely forgotten (in my prospectus it was stated that assays of ore and analyses of minerals, &c., would be most carefully conducted, and all business of the kind attended to, with great steadiness and despatch); and pending the advent of work, the scene of my future operations was enlivened by athletic sport and every kind of jollification, which helped me to endure the anxiety of my parents at seeing me start on the serious business of life so young." He goes on to say that, thanks to kindness of friends of his family, employment came: he was given an order for analysing various specimens of soil from a friend's estate. "I conducted these experiments with proper earnestness, and he paid me for them with becoming gravity. I now thank him kindly for the same (it would have been undignified to do so then) and sincerely hope that he has found my scientific research beneficial to his land." Then the gold contagion suddenly broke out and committed great ravages. "I caught it one rainy afternoon near the Exchange; my mother and sister instantly became affected, but my father, who was of a stout habit and robust temperament, and gifted with a very practical turn of mind, fortunately escaped, and devoted himself to our cure. Thanks to his judicious nursing, I was the first to recover." "The gold fever raged worse and worse, and I waited impatiently for it to give me employment; at length it did so, in a few months from the period of its birth: somebody introduced me to somebody else, who introduced me to the chairman of the Victoria Gold and Copper Mine, situated near Moleville, in Blankshire."

Then follows an interview with the directors. "It was necessary that in my interview with the directors next day, I should cram them with every possible technical term that had ever been invented for the purpose."

He manages to squeeze "lodes," "gossans," "costeanings," and other impressive words into almost every sentence. It produces a great effect on the directors.

The offer of a guinea and a half a day to go down the mine inspires a wild impulse to embrace the whole board in the person of the venerable fat old fellow who makes the offer. This is restrained. "I told him I would think of the matter, and return him an answer the following day; and, after bouncing myself first into the office-clerk and then into the fire-place, I eventually succeeded in making an unconcerned exit."

"I pass over my triumphant sensations and the family bliss, only chequered by anxiety lest the Victoria Gold and Copper Mine should come to grief before I got there."

He then travels through enchanting scenery, and is conducted to the mine. "Some five and twenty or thirty shaggy rough-looking men were about. These were the miners. Their appearance was not reassuring, and when the engineer left me alone with them, with a parting injunction that I was to make them feel I had an iron will at once, I confess I felt myself uncomfortably young, and a little bit at a loss.

"We proceeded to business at once, however; and as I met their first little symptoms of insubordination with one or two acts of summary justice (which I will spare the reader, but which, emanating from me, caused me unlimited astonishment), I soon established a proper authority over them, and we thenceforward got on together capitally."

We are then given extracts from a mining diary—significantly left off at a particular stage of the proceedings—used as a sketch-book. An unfavourable report as to the finding of gold is sent in to the board.

"The miners did not believe in the mine, and as they perceived that I did not either, they believed in me to a most flattering extent." He soon got very much attached to the miners, and used to tell stories about foreign lands while they were distilling the pure mercury, or performing other innocent operations suggested by the board, enlightening them on various subjects where he felt their ignorance to be equal to his own. "My letters home contained descriptions and sketches of them, and my mamma became interested in their spiritual welfare." Surrounded by the halo of memory, they afterwards seemed to him primitive gentlemen worthy of King Arthur's Round Table. He describes existence between the hours of work as full of charm owing to the friendship of surrounding farmers and small gentry. In a "Trilby" way he describes how he "rode, and wrestled, and boxed with them! and fell in love with their sisters, and sketched them, and sang Tyrolese melodies to them, ... blessing the lucky stroke of fortune which had made him mining engineer to a gold mine without any gold, and managed by gentlemen who obstinately persisted in ignoring the latter important fact, in spite of his honest endeavours to persuade them of it." "I have," he says, "only to hum a certain 'jodel' chorus, and the whole scene returns to me, surrounded by that peculiar fascination which belongs to past pleasures—a phenomenon far more interesting to me than the most marvellous phenomenon of science."

Every artist is an experimental psychologist, the material for his art is really always some mental experience. He wishes to communicate with his public in the spirit of this experience. With Scott it was the old associations of places, with du Maurier the associations of "old times," of personal memory. This was the frame of mind the interpretation of which absorbed him in his literary art, distinguishing it, except in his early *Cornhill* work, from his art with the pencil.

There is not much in the remaining part of the gold-mine narrative which can be shown to bear upon the artist's career. The conclusion of the story shows his forfeiture of the regard of the directors by openness of speech to the shareholders as to the proceedings at the mine.

Such was his experience of a mine in Devonshire and of relationship with the miners, who, with the limited experience of the mining classes in those days, had some difficulty in "placing" du Maurier with his, to them, unusual physical delicacy and yet more unusual personal charm.

§ 4

The literary gift in the above narration will, we think, be evident even in our quotations. But during the greater part of his life du Maurier's literary gift remained unknown to the general public, though more than one editor under whom he served on *Punch* urged him to take a writer's salary and be on the literary as well as on the artistic staff. It was said that he relied with comfort upon this second talent to support him in the event of his sight failing him altogether. There was a space of thirty years between the above contribution to *Once a Week* and the writing of his first novel, *Peter Ibbetson*. But it is in that novel that he again returns to the story of his career, through boyhood and youth, leading up to the period in which his father started him in the laboratory.

Du Maurier had in 1856, when his father died, practically the choice of two arts, painting and singing, in both of which he seemed to have a chance of distinguishing himself. And as the essay of 1861 was so soon afterwards to prove, there was really another alternative, that of authorship, for the gifted analytical chemist. He decided then to forsake the chemistry to which he had been trained, but remained undecided about everything else.

In 1856, at the age of twenty-two, he returned to Paris with his mother, to live in the Rue Paradis-Poissonière, very poor, very dull, and very miserable, as he himself has said; but almost at the entrance of what he describes as the best time of his life—that period in which, deciding to follow art as a profession, he entered the studio of Gleyre. Those were the joyous Quartier Latin days. He has described Gleyre's studio in *Trilby*. The happy life there lasted a year: Whistler and Poynter, as is well known, were his fellow-students.

The studio of Gleyre was inherited from Delaroche, and afterwards handed down to Gerome. Whistler, Poynter, du Maurier, Lamont, and Thomas Armstrong were the group of *Trilby*, Lamont was "the Laird," Aleco Ionides "the Greek," and Rowley is supposed to have been "Taffy."[4]

86

HONOUR WHERE HONOUR IS DUE

SIR GORGIUS MIDAS (WHO HAS NOT BEEN MADE A PEER).
"WHY, IT'S ENOUGH TO MAKE A MAN TURN RADICAL,
'ANGED IF IT AIN'T, TO THINK OF SICH SERVICES AS MINE
BEIN' REWARDED WITH NO 'IGHER TITLE THAN WHAT'S
BESTOWED ON A HEMINENT SAWBONES, OR A HINGERNEER,
OR A LITTERY MAN, OR EVEN A SUCCESSFUL HARTIST!"

MRS. PONSONBY DE TOMKYNS (SYMPATHETICALLY). "IT
DOES SEEM HARD! BUT YOU'VE ONLY TO BIDE YOUR TIME,
SIR GORGIUS. NO MAN OF YOUR STAMP NEED EVER DESPAIR
OF A PEERAGE!" (AND MRS. PONSONBY DE TOMKYNS IS, AS
USUAL, QUITE RIGHT.)

PUNCH, MAY 15, 1880.

In 1857 du Maurier went on to the Antwerp Academy, where the
masters were De Keyser and Van Lerins. It was in the latter's studio
that the disaster of his life occurred. He was drawing from a model,
when suddenly the girl's head seemed to him to dwindle to the size
of a walnut. He clapped his hand over his left eye, and wondered if
he had been mistaken. He could see as well as ever. But when in its
turn he covered his right eye he learned what had happened. His left

eye had failed him. It might be altogether lost. It grew worse, until the fear of blindness overtook him. In the spring of 1859 he went to a specialist in Dusseldorf, who, while deciding that the left eye was lost, said that with care there was no reason to fear losing the other. Du Maurier was never able to shake off the terror of apprehension. He was apparently a hopeless invalid at Christmas-time in 1859, "in some dreary, deserted, dismal Flemish town," in hospital. Turning over *Punch's Almanack,* the delight the paper afforded him in such unhappy circumstances was "a thing not to be forgotten." It fired him with a new ambitious dream. The astonishing thing was that before another year was over the dream was beginning to come true: he was in England, making friends with Keene, who introduced him to John Leech, whom he was destined to succeed at *Punch's* table.

The artist left Antwerp in 1860, and for several months he and Whistler lived together in Newman Street. Their studio has been described. Stretched across it was a rope like a clothes-line, from which floated a bit of brocade, their curtain to shut off the corner used as a bedroom. There was hardly even a chair to sit on, and often with the brocade a towel hung from the line.

§ 5

In the autumn of 1860 the artist began to contribute to *Once a Week.* Then followed a contribution to *Punch* for which he continued to draw as an occasional contributor chiefly of initial letters and the like, until he reached the stage of contributing regular "Pictures" with legends beneath in 1864. It was not until 1865, however, that his full pages in *Punch* became frequent. In that year he succeeded Leech at the *Punch* table.

His career practically began with his marriage to Miss Emma Wightwick. Following the example of his master, Thackeray, he courageously married upon "prospects," as soon as ever the promise of regular employment for his pencil seemed to be secure. This was the year in which he illustrated Mrs. Gaskell's *Sylvia's Lovers.* "My life," he once said, "was a very prosperous one from the outset in London; I was married in 1863, and my wife and I never once knew financial troubles. My only trouble has been my fear about my eyes. Apart from that I have been very happy."

Upon marrying, du Maurier moved to Great Russell Street, and, later, to rooms in Earl's Terrace, Kensington, the house where Walter Pater died.

In the days when he was living in Great Russell Street the journalistic world of London was very Bohemian. It is true that Leech had not made a good Bohemian, but it was not until some time after du Maurier's accession to the *Punch* table that the weekly dinner lost an uproarious gaiety that is recognised as the true Bohemian note. Mr. Punch and his staff all improved their tone, Bohemia is now only a memory. It is the very genius of Mr. Punch that makes him respond to the moment and become the most decorous figure in the world in decorous times.

One cannot help being struck by a resemblance between the coming to town and the almost immediate success there of du Maurier and Thackeray. The comparison has its interest in the fact that as every man has his master, beyond all dispute Thackeray was du Maurier's master. Both quitted Bohemia, but in Society always retained the detachment of artists. It was near to Thackeray's initials that du Maurier was destined to cut his own on the great *Punch* table. He himself described the glamour Thackeray's name possessed for him, inspiring him as he climbed out of the despair that followed the sudden partial deprivation of his sight. The only time he met his master he was too diffident to accept an invitation to be introduced. Thackeray seemed so great. But all that evening he remained as close to him as possible, greedily listening to his words. Like Thackeray, du Maurier thought that the finest thing in the world was to live without fear and without reproach. It is probable that Thackeray would not at all have minded not being taken for a genius, but he would violently have resented not being accounted a gentleman. For him that implied the great heart and the scrupulous honour which Bohemia does not insist upon if you have great spirits.

§ 6

Of du Maurier's great friendship with Canon Ainger, which commenced in the seventies, light is to be obtained from Edith Sichel's *Life and Letters of Alfred Ainger*.[5]

CANON AINGER
PORTRAIT IN WATER-COLOUR BY DU MAURIER. IN THE
POSSESSION OF THE ARTIST'S WIDOW.

"For fifteen years," says Miss Sichel, "they always met once, and generally twice a day. Hampstead knew their figures as every afternoon they walked round the pond on the Heath, deep in conversation. Edward Fitzgerald himself never had a closer friendship than had these two men for one another. Their mental climates suited; they were akin, yet had strong differences. Perhaps in the quickness of their mutual attraction Frenchman recognised Frenchman. But Ainger was the French Huguenot and du Maurier the French sceptic. Both had mercurial perceptions, and exercised them on much the same objects. Both were wits and humorists, but Ainger was more of a wit than a humorist, and du Maurier was more of a humorist than a wit. Both were men of fancy rather than of imagination, men of sentiment rather than of passion. Both, too, were fantastics; both loved what was beautiful and graceful rather than what was grand; but du Maurier was more of the pure artist, while to Ainger the moral side of beauty most appealed.... Both men were gifted with an exquisite kindness.... Du Maurier was the keener and clearer thinker of the two; he had the wider outlook and the fewer prejudices." Their closest bond was *Punch,* which was to Ainger a delight from cover to cover.

The artist's love of Whitby is well known; he expressed it himself in his *Punch* drawings over and over again. He wrote to Ainger in 1891: "It is delightful to get a letter from you at Whitby—the place we all like best in the world." He gives a list of places and things to be especially seen there, among them the cottage of Sylvia Robson of *Sylvia's Lovers,* and No 1 St. Hilda's Terrace, "the humble but singularly charming little house where your friends have dwelt, and would fain dwell again (and two of them end their days there, somewhere towards the middle of the twentieth century)."

It was at Whitby when Ainger and his nieces were there with the du Mauriers that they were once delighted by seeing "Trilby Drops" advertised in a little village sweet-shop. "Such is fame," said du Maurier, but when his daughter went in to ask about the "drops," the girl behind the counter had no idea what "Trilby" meant.

In the summer numbers of past volumes of *Punch* Whitby has figured in the background of seaside scenes perhaps more than any other watering-place. Du Maurier nearly always drew upon it for seaside pictures and the humour of the summer holidays. He formed his first acquaintance with it in illustrating *Sylvia's Lovers.* The scene of that tale is Whitby under another name. Thus he started his connection with the town in circumstances that seemed to him to give it a glamour. Not only did he confess an immense liking for Mrs. Gaskell's novel, but, as we have seen, he scored in the illustration of it the first of his great successes with the general public. The gift of illustration, after all, is a very rare one. Nothing is to be understood more easily than the value the public began to put upon du Maurier's gift. In a response of that sort the public display true discrimination. The ascendency of du Maurier as a *Punch* artist was more than anything due to the fact that for his work in that paper he drew upon the sentiment of family life from the resources of his own experience. And nothing that we could write here would so entirely reveal the happy character of his own family life as the reigning atmosphere of the "seaside" and "nursery" pictures which he contributed to *Punch*.

§ 7

Many people remembering du Maurier's satires entertained a little fear of him in Society, and of what he might be thinking about them. An instance of this was shown on one occasion when he was dining alone with Sir John Millais at the latter's splendid residence. "I suppose," said Millais, waving his hand in the direction of the disappearing flunkeys after dinner, "you think all this very *Sir Gorgius Midas-y*? To me it is merely respectable." As a matter of fact there is everything to show that du Maurier entertained the same sort of notions of "respectability" as his host, though he did things on a less magnificent scale. By temperament he was not quite a Bohemian, although he was convivial. It was the convivial side of the weekly *Punch* dinner that appealed to him. He abstained from these meetings, or came in late, when a tendency prevailed to make them too much, as he thought, the pretext of business. He was regarded as singular in ordering an immense cup of tea to be put before him immediately after dinner. He sat over his cup of tea with a bent back, always with a cigarette, fuming whilst the business part of the proceedings went forward. When that was over he entered into his own, regaling his comrades with droll stories, creating a witty atmosphere at his own corner by his taste for repartee.

THE MUTUAL ADMIRATIONISTS

(FRAGMENTS OVERHEARD BY GRIGSBY AND THE COLONEL AT ONE OF PRIGSBY'S AFTERNOON TEAS.)

YOUNG MAUDLE (TO MRS. LYON HUNTER AND HER DAUGHTERS). "IN THE SUPREMEST POETRY, SHAKESPEARE'S FOR INSTANCE, OR POSTLETHWAITE'S, OR SHELLEY'S ONE ALWAYS FEELS THAT," &C., &C., &C.

YOUNG POSTLETHWAITE (TO THE THREE MISS BILDERBOGIES). "THE GREATEST PAINTERS OF ALL, SUCH AS VELASQUEZ, OR MAUDLE, OR EVEN TITIAN, INVARIABLY SUGGEST TO ONE," &C., &C., &C.

PUNCH, MAY 22, 1880.

The difficulties with his sight might well have been expected to poison the artist's well of happiness. But it was noticed of Charles Lamb that the very fact of possessing the little pleasures of everyday life only under a lease, as it were, which Fate at any moment might refuse to renew, caused him to be the very poet of such pleasures, experiencing them with an acuteness that became to him an inspiration. With du Maurier the enjoyment of social life, so manifestly evident in his art at one time, may well have been entered into with something of the fierce delight with which we take our sunshine in a rainy summer. In later years he became home-staying in his habits. One imagines he felt that he had taken from Society all that it had to give him—the knowledge of life necessary to him in his work, and friends in sufficient number. It is from about this time that his art shows evidence that an intimate contact with the social movement was no longer sustained. The tendency to repeat himself, to produce his weekly picture by a sort of formula, becomes noticeable; and the absence of variety in his work becomes oppressive.

Du Maurier was a man of great natural versatility. For some reason or other he was not fond of the theatre, but he was in possession of a considerable genius for monodrama, and often delighted his friends by his impersonations. We have seen that it was once within the bounds of possibility that he would have become a professional singer. His conversational gifts were great. He was a writer of singular picturesqueness. A considerable interest in the progress of science was noted in him to the last. If we look back at the record of the lives of artists to find what manner of men as a rule they were, we shall find that, in contradistinction to poets and musicians, they were pre-eminent as men of the world. Skill in plastic art seems a final gift imparted to men very highly constituted. It steals them entirely away from other aims, but exists side by side with, while yet it transcends the ability to achieve remarkable performances in dissimilar directions. Perhaps it is because, of all men, the true artist regards the material world with the clearest vision, living in no world of dreams, finding reality itself so delightful.

The artist never at any stage of his life lost the rollicking spirit of a boy. It broke out in conversation and in his letters. In narration he reserved the right of every *raconteur* to make a point by some exaggeration. In letters of his that I have seen the note of high spirits may be said to be the prevailing one.

For instance, to the head of the *Punch* Firm, after a *Punch* dinner:

"*Jan.* 14.

"Would you allow one of your retainers to look under the table and see if I left a golosh there—and if so, tell him to leave it at Swain's, to be returned by his messenger on Monday? I must have been tight, and the golosh not tight enough, and I appeared at the Duchess's with one golosh and my trousers tucked up. H.R.H. was much concerned about it, and said, 'It's all that — — *Punch* dinner!'"

To the same:

"I'm on for the 25th at the Albion and much delighted. Is it evening dress? If not, tip us a card. If you do not I shall conclude it is, and appear in full togs, which I will get out for the evening.

(Attenborough)

"I had really hoped to have got down to Bouverie Street yesterday, but the conviction forced itself on me as the day wore on that I should never get a cab to bring me back. I know I am a back-slider in the matter of the *Punch* dinner (and all other dinners when I can help it). I can get thro' my work so much better after the frugal home repast, and in bed before 11 P.M. Not that I have been able to indulge in the early couch these holidays, for Hampstead, slow as it is, is a fearful place for juvenile dissipation, and parents have to sit up night after night at Xmas time. I hope you Wandsworthians have more sense."

In an earlier stage of the book we fixed the period at which du Maurier's work in *Punch* was at the height of its vitality at about

1879—and on into the early "eighties." And the artist himself seems to have had a strong feeling of increasing power at this time. In January 1880 he approached *Punch* for a revision of the prices at which he was then working. By the courtesy of Mr. W. Laurence Bradbury I am able to quote in part from letters bearing out the inference that it was at this time that du Maurier entered into consciousness of his own worth:

"*Jan.* 1, 1880.

"DEAR BRADBURY, AGNEW, & Co.,—The time has come when I think I may fairly ask you to make an increase in my salary.

"The quality of my work has greatly improved of late years and my popularity has grown in proportion, and these results have been obtained at great expense of thought and labour, and I find as a rule that the more time I devote to each production, the more favour it meets with from the public.

"It is now a good many years (seven or eight I believe) since you were kind enough at my request to raise the payment of the quarter page....

"Since that period I have gradually become enabled thro' the improvement in my health to give much more of my time to my *Punch* work—all the drawings selected by you for 'English Society at Home' have been done since then—and whatever other qualities they may possess, they are very careful and elaborate in most instances, and without this care and elaboration they would lose most of their value in the world's eye...."

Then follows details as to the revision of the prices. And then a day or two later he sends the following letter:

"*Jan.* 4, 1880.

"Mr DEAR BRADBURY,—Many thanks for your kind note. It is really a painful effort to me to 'ask for more,' and I've been putting it off from day to day these six months. The pleasure and enthusiasm with which I have got to do my work for *Punch* (since I have got better in health and so forth) are such that I should be content to go on so for ever, without any rise, if it weren't for my having such a deuce of a family! but what's a fellow to do!

"You've no idea what it is to go trapesing up and down, hunting for a subject, *while all the time the hand remains idle. Punch* requires such a lot of thought, you see — and then when the time comes for the hand to do its work, you can see what care and time are taken with the execution....

"I only wish it would suit the convenience of *Punch* to take all the work I could send on a scale of prices literally fixed by myself! (ye modern Hogarth!! 10,000,000 a year! R.A. — P.R.A. — Sir George!!!)"

At the foot of this letter is a thumb-nail picture of "Chang," du Maurier's huge Newfoundland, leading a blind man, initialled D.M. The dog holds a tin and begs from a passing fine lady, a well-known beauty of Society and the Stage, and the legend "Sic transit Gloria Mundi" describes the situation.

§ 8

The above letters were dated from New Grove House, Hampstead, where the du Mauriers lived for twenty-one years. They had moved into this house from Church Row, where they had gone when they first came to Hampstead, and where their youngest son was born. During the period of their long residence in New Grove House they frequently took a furnished house for the winter season in Town for the convenience of going into Society. It was the inaccessibility of Hampstead before the days of the Hampstead Tube that made du Maurier latterly relinquish many social engagements, and developed the disinclination for theatre-going which I have seen ascribed to an aversion from the drama.

Sir Frederick Wedmore says that it was at Hampstead evening parties that du Maurier found his type of the Adonis up-to-date. Alas, that even by Sir Frederick Wedmore the type should be regarded as salient of du Maurier's pictures. It is further evidence that the artist is only remembered by his later pictures. It is in these the type monotonously appears. But we feel better disposed towards Hampstead when the eminent critic adds that Church Row itself gave du Maurier more than one of the models in whom one recognises his ideal of youthful feminine charm.

Du Maurier's tastes were very quiet. His interests were centred in his home, and he found no companionship more acceptable than that of his own children. He was not at all fond of being alone. He preferred even to work with people round him; writing his novels in the drawing-room standing with the MS. upon the top of the piano, and walking up and down undisturbed by the conversation of his family round him. It caused him no annoyance when members of his family broke into his studio during working hours. His work both as draughtsman and writer was always produced without any of that pathetic travail which for many artists and writers lies between conception and expression. He did not exhibit the most unpleasant of the traits of a talented person—the overstrung condition of nerves which makes a man unpleasant to a household; he preserved the serenity that pertains to greater genius still. His house was always an open one, and the life in it must have been highly typical of that English family life of which he was the pre-eminent poet in his drawings.

MANUSCRIPT OF "NOCTURNE"

"SUN OF THE SLEEPLESS—MELANCHOLY STAR!"—BYRON.

TRANSLATED INTO FRENCH BY GEORGE DU MAURIER.

THE ENGLISH ILLUSTRATED MAGAZINE, SEPTEMBER 13, 1886.

Du Maurier was elected a member of the Athenæum Club under Rule 2. He showed his appreciation of this Club by not making use of any other, though he was such a highly sociable man. He was early a member of the Arts Club, though using it less frequently after its removal to the Dover Street house, of old-world distinction. At the Athenæum he frequented the billiard-room as a sociable place, though he was not very fond of billiards or card games. He could get on quite well in life upon "conversation" as a recreation, interspersed with music.

After the great *Trilby* boom, and when he was writing *The Martian*—in fact, only a year before his death, the artist moved into town to live in Oxford Square. He was partly influenced in this by the expiration of the twenty-one years' lease upon which he held the Hampstead property.

In a paper contributed to the *Hampstead Annual* for 1897, the issue following the artist's death, Canon Ainger traced various Hampstead spots to be identified as the backgrounds of du Maurier's subjects, and recalls how on Hampstead Heath many subjects for *Punch* came to be discussed between them in the course of conversation. He describes the way that one of the artist's most famous jests, in the days of Maudle and Postlethwaite, took its final shape one day in Hampstead, and by a singular chance arose out of a University sermon at Cambridge.

A certain well-known humorist of the time had remarked that the objection to Blue China (it was the special craze at the moment) was that it was so difficult to "live up to it." This utterance had been lately taken somewhat over-seriously by a special preacher before the University who, discoursing on the growing extravagances and frivolities of the age, wound up an indignant tirade by an eloquent peroration to the effect that things had come to a sad pass when persons were found to talk of "*living up*—to a Tea-pot." At this juncture the jest seemed ripe for treatment, and du Maurier thereupon produced his famous drawing of the æsthetic bride and bridegroom comparing notes over the precious piece of crockery in question: "Oh! Algernon! Let us live up to it!"

Speaking of fifteen years of constant companionship in walks upon the Heath, the Canon says no one could have had a better opportunity of tasting the unfailing charm of du Maurier's conversation, the width of his reading and observation, and his inexhaustible fund of anecdote. In these conversations Canon Ainger heard every detail of his companion's school life, his studio-life in Paris, which afterwards found a place in the pages of his three novels.

Referring to the long years of uninterrupted achievement of the artist's life at Hampstead, "only once," says his friend, "in all the years I knew him was he forced to lay his pencil by for a season. His solitary eye had temporarily failed him, but, with spirits unsubdued, he promptly took up the art of lecturer with marked success, although from the first it was against the grain. When, however, after an interval his sight returned to him, and the literary instinct, encouraged doubtless by the success of his lectures, began to quicken, he gained, we all know, though then past fifty years of age, a new public and a new career in writing fiction." "Except," proceeds Canon Ainger, "to his intimate friends and to his colleagues on *Punch* the display of this gift was an absolute surprise.... He wrote with extraordinary and even dangerous facility. It is fair, however, to add that his best passages were often produced as rapidly as all the rest. For instance, the scene in *Trilby* when the mother and uncle of Little Billee arrive in Paris, hearing of the engagement, and have their first interview with Taffy, was written straight off one evening between dinner and bed-time." This scene, in the judgment of Ainger, represents du Maurier at his high-water mark as a novelist and as a worthy follower of the great master on whom his style was undoubtedly based.

"Hampstead," continues the Canon, "was a real foster-mother to George du Maurier, not only in what it brought him but in what it saved him from. He was by nature and by practice one of the most generous and hospitable of men. He loved to entertain his friends from town, and to take them afterwards his favourite walks. But he disliked dinners and evening parties in London, not because he was unsociable, but because good dinners and long journeys 'took it out of him' and endangered the task of the following morning. The distance from town and the long hills made late hours inevitable. To listen to some new book read aloud in the studio, which was also the common sitting-room of wife and children, made the chief happiness of his evening."

"We owed it," says his friend, "to Hampstead air with its many sylvan beauties that du Maurier was able for so long, notwithstanding defective sight and health gradually failing, to prosecute his daily work with scarce an interruption."

The link between the place and the work produced in it is in the case of du Maurier, apart from the fact that Hampstead scenes so frequently recur in his pictures, anything but a superficial one. "Hampstead," the artist wrote, "is healthy but dull." It was the very monotony of the place, the even conditions under which it was possible to work there in his day—when it was farther away than it is in the present age of "tubes"—that assisted the building up of the remarkable record in *Punch*—the indispensable contribution made every week by du Maurier to the journalism which, in the days when the fashionable world counted several influential journals devoted to itself, placed *Punch* in its unique position among them. Society reserved quite a touching deference for the opinions of Mr. Punch. It gives us some idea of the position into which the paper had worked itself a generation ago when we find Ruskin, the greatest social critic of his day, going straight to it for an authoritative picture of the time. People have not sufficiently remembered how often when they have referred to *Punch* they were really referring to du Maurier, or what is left now of his tradition—his way of dealing with the foibles of society. The position of the paper in Society was won by appositeness of political criticism, and the delicate edge of its satire. It was du Maurier who put that edge on. Society returned fascinated after every wound to inspect the weapon. Keene's pen brought immense artistic prestige to *Punch*, but its social prestige it owes to du Maurier more than to anyone; we only become aware that Leech had begun a tradition in its pages by its supreme fulfilment in du Maurier's art.

§ 9

Henry Silver, a member of the *Punch* staff, who came to the table in 1858, kept a diary of the talk of the table until he retired in 1870. The present writer was the more touched by the honour of being permitted to look into this interesting document from the fact that the pen of the exquisite E.V. Lucas has but lately inspired itself at the same source. This was for a paper of Thackerayana which concluded, after reference to the death of Leech, Thackeray's friend: "On November 7th (1864) Leech's successor, George du Maurier, took his seat at the Table, and so the world goes on."

GEORGE DU MAURIER
FROM A PHOTOGRAPH.

Thackeray bulks more largely in the diary than even du Maurier, for du Maurier's genius in the table conversation was wholly for asides. We have already mentioned his comparative lack of interest in the debates over the large cartoon. And this Silver himself draws attention to: "Du M. and H.S. generally mute when the 'L.C.' is discussed." The conversation at each meeting is for some time closely confined to the discussion of the cartoon, then it spreads to every imaginable topic. One feels that one assists at the making of history when the Great Cartoon, or Cut, as they called it, is discussed—as, for instance, when the design for the one representing Disraeli on the side of the Angels is decided upon, after his famous speech at Oxford in 1864. The desultory conversation reported in the diary on each occasion after settlement of the cartoon throws a light upon things uppermost in the public mind at the time. It is noted when the Queen comes out of retirement into the world again. And a vivid reflection is to be found of the horror felt at the news of the assassination of Lincoln. Men as closely united as the *Punch* staff have prejudices as clearly defined as those of an individual. There was great hostility to the Swinburne of the sixties. Du Maurier on one occasion sticks up for Swinburne as "the writer of lovely verses—the weaver of words—the rhymer of rhymes." "Du M. and H.S. agree in thinking Tennyson will live 'chiefly by his songs and minor lays.'"

"Du M. thinks *Vanity Fair* a little Bible," "Rather an epistle by the Corinthians," says Shirley Brooks.

One night after dinner du Maurier walked home in the wet. "My carriage is waiting for Silver," he said. "My carriage is waiting for gold," answered Shirley Brooks.

Sometimes the discourse at the table is of Religion. "Du M. believes in God, and that whatever we do God will not punish us."

"A comfortable faith," adds Silver.

Once the discussion turned upon suicide. "Du M. says before he married he often felt tempted to suicide."

In heading his diary shortly after du Maurier joined the table, Silver writes "Du M." and then corrects it "(no: DU M.)." And in another place he writes, "Du Maurier says fellows write to him de Maurier: 'give the devil his du.'"

In 1865 the proprietors, getting old, have put their sons in their stead, and taken the Agnews into partnership. The staff talk sentimentally of old times. They drink success to the Firm. Mark Lemon, the Editor, proposes the health of Bradbury & Evans, saying, "men work well together because they are liberally treated. Thought our loss last year (death of Leech) would have seriously affected *Punch*, but it did not. And no single loss will." Bradbury, replying, speaks of the brotherly affection between the editor and the proprietors. "Says if you want men to serve you well treat them well, and win their sympathy and esteem.... Evans is emphatic on the Brotherhood of the Punch table." Thackeray's "Mahogany Tree" is sung; du Maurier sings a French song, and F.C.B. also singeth a song with no words to speak of, &c. &c. &c. "So we pass a jolly evening, and bear in mind — that Sociality is the secret of the success of *Punch*."

On another occasion there is the paper's "Silver Wedding." A watch and chain with eleven links—the mystic number of the *Punch* staff— is handed over to Mark Lemon. In the morning he has received a letter with a hundred guineas. He claims, in replying, "that the *Punch* Brotherhood is one of the most extraordinary literary brotherhoods the world has seen."

Shirley Brooks hands him letters written by the staff individually, testifying their gladness at the gift proposed. Du Maurier wrote the longest and Charles Keene the shortest.

We have extracted the following items from the diary, quoting exactly, except for the substitution sometimes of the full name for initials:

November 7th—Monday. "S.B., du Maurier (his début), H.S., J.T., M.L., P.L., F.C.B., H.M., T.T.

"(The initials stand for Shirley Brooks, Henry Silver, John Tenniel, Mark Lemon, Professor Leigh, F.C. Burnand, Horace Mayhew, Tom Taylor.)

"Du Maurier tells of Whistler and Rossetti's rage for old china, and how Rossetti once left his guests at dinner and rushed off to buy a piece before Whistler could forestall him."

May 17, 1865. "Du Maurier was presented with a son and heir on Saturday, so we baptized the infant in a bumper of Champagne."

December 20, 1865. "While the Great Cut is being hatched, Burnand, du Maurier, and Silver all make little cuts of their initials on the *Punch* table. Henry Silver between William Thackeray and John Leech—Burnand where à Beckett sat and du Maurier where Leech."

"Miss Bateman retired from the stage (at Her Majesty's) on Friday— she has rather proved herself a one-part actress, and so has Sothern, whom Burnand denounces as a practical joker—most unscrupulous in tongue."

"Du M. thinks it harder to write a poem than to paint a picture. But surely there's no comparing them. One mind expresses itself with a pen and another with a brush."

Jan. 17, 1866. "Du Maurier tells of the gas blow-up at his 91 Great Russell Street on Boxing-day. Girl dressing in the shop for Hairdressers' Ball—turned on two burners and lit one and left it burning. Du Maurier and wife dressing on top floor—bang! like a hundred pounder, and then rattle—smash—crash. 'O! the children!' 'D—n it! They're all right!' first time he ever swore before his wife. Sister tried to jump from window, but Armstrong held her back. Baby crowing in his arms at the fun as he came downstairs. The nursemaids had run away of course. Lucky no one on the stairs, or they'd have been killed."

April 4, 1866. "In reference to a Ball on the Haymarket stage— 'Would you like to go?' said S.B. to du Maurier. But du Maurier's dancing days are over—only cares for dinners now! Fancy the old fogydom of thirty!"

November 7, 1868. "Du Maurier cut down to five cigarettes a day, resolves to ride daily and live frugally: frightened by his eye this summer!!"

February 24, 1868. "Tenniel has almost given up smoking! Used to smoke an ounce a day. Can eat a better breakfast now. Nearly all our *Punch* folk smoke less. Tom Taylor has given up cigars and only takes a pipe occasionally. Du Maurier takes cigarettes four a day in lieu of forty. H.S. never smokes at all after dinner. Only Keene and Mark and Shirley stick to their tobacco."

§ 10

Sir Francis Burnand, till recently the distinguished Editor of *Punch*, was du Maurier's senior on the paper by a year or two. He has very kindly sent the writer the following impression of the artist: "That he was beloved as a cheery, witty *confrère*, goes without saying. Rarely did he mix himself up with politics in any shape or form. I doubt if he ever gave us any assistance in devising a political cartoon. What his politics were I am unable to say, and I do not think he troubled himself about the matter. In 'the old days' he delighted in chaffing Horace Mayhew, with whom he exchanged 'slang' in French. With the jovial proprietor, William Bradbury, he was always on the best of terms of friendly nonsense, being invariably his left-hand neighbour at 'The Table.' He was a genuine Bohemian of the artistic fraternity (as given in his *Trilby*) with the true polish of an English gentleman, of the kindest disposition, and of the warmest heart. All who knew him well loved him, and none missed him more than his fellow-workers on *Punch*."

"His religion," Sir Francis volunteered in a further note, "as that of the majority of his French *confrères*, you will find it in the artistic sketches of the men and women in *La Bohème*" "His guardian angel, humanly and socially, was his wife."

Everyone who knew du Maurier now speaks of his attractiveness and the simplicity and honesty of his nature. He was not really very fond of "Society" because of its code of insincerity. He was its satirist for the same reason that, much as he liked "to be with people," he was not at-home where manners were affected. The Victorians who survive to this day hold up their hands in horror at present-day manners; they object to our natural, comfortable ways and clothes; they define our naturalness as laziness. But just because it is so constitutional to be lazy, the casual modern manners, so true to the exact shade of our enthusiasm for, or indifference to any particular person or thing, express our virtue. We are too honest to pretend. We look back with amusement to the Victorians, who put all their goods in the shop window, whose very movements were so far without freedom as to be subservient to the maintenance of uncreased clothing. A regard for "appearances" seemed to regulate action. It was an age of *poseurs*—the age of the "professional air." In that age came into use among doctors "the bedside manner." Shop-walkers then distinguished themselves from the rest of the race by their preposterous antics, artists endured the misery of velvet jackets; women tight-laced, men about town invented the crease in the trouser-leg to keep which in order alone demands the fealty of a lifetime. In summer men consented to be roasted alive on the London pavement rather than part with the frock-coat in which their depraved conception of beauty delighted. In those days one imagines people were only comfortable when once safely in bed, and that was never for long at a time; for the sake of appearances the Victorians got up early.

SPEED THE PARTING GUEST

(THINGS ONE WOULD RATHER HAVE LEFT UNSAID.)

"WE'VE HAD SUCH A PLEASANT EVENING, MR. JONES! MAY I BEG OF YOU TO ASK ONE OF YOUR SERVANTS TO CALL A HANSOM?"

"WITH PLEASURE, MRS. SMITH!"

PUNCH, MARCH 10, 1883.

The Royal Academy Exhibitions of the time proved that it was impossible for a Victorian to be an artist. The artists of the time did not belong to their own age. We had Rossetti ever seeking to lose himself in the illusion of another time and country, and Whistler trying to find himself in the reality of another place. Chelsea was well outside of Victorian London. Perhaps Hampstead, a place like Chelsea, that belongs to no particular time, was outside of it too. Kensington and Bayswater are Victorian to this day. Rossetti in Kensington is a vision from which imagination recoils, Whistler in Bayswater one which passes the invention of human fancy. Du Maurier liked to come into Victorian London in a carriage from a distance, as a visitor, to be driven away again. He approached its society critically. He acknowledged the distinction of its grave self-consciousness while exposing its ridiculous airs.

Just as Chelsea is a more desirable place to live in because of its "Rossetti" associations, so Hampstead gains from the memory of the witty and generous satirist who made it his home. New Grove House, where du Maurier lived for over twenty years, might have been designed for him; it escapes the suburban style that would have been an affliction to one so romantic.

Nearly all artists who have sustained their powers in a refined field of expression have been glad to count upon monotony in the passage of their days. The adventurous temperament is not the artistic one. The artist values security from interruptions above everything, and interruption is of the essence of adventure. Du Maurier lived a life that was for an artist characteristic. He was at pains to preserve his days from being broken into. It is above the plane where human life is open to crude forms of calamity and the stress of elemental passion, upon a plane where freedom from anxiety is secure that art is able to exert itself in attaining to the expression of the more valuable, because more intimate, experiences of human nature.

Du Maurier died on the 8th October 1896. His grave at Hampstead is singularly happily placed and constructed. It consists of two carved wood crosses, respectively at head and foot, connected by a panel containing, in addition to the name and dates, only the concluding lines of *Trilby*:—

> "A little trust that when we die
> We reap our sowing! And so—good-bye!"

The grave is close to the pavement, and it is impossible to go that way without seeing it. We can imagine that one who was so entirely the opposite of misanthropic would wish to lie like this within sound of passing conversation.

FOOTNOTES:

[4] Pennell's *Life of Whistler*.

[5] Archibald Constable & Co.

V

THE ILLUSTRATIONS

§1

It may be well to touch upon some of the characteristics of our illustrations in detail before closing this book. Many of them are so obviously involved in what has already been said here of the artist's work that we do not propose to mention them again; but others suggest remarks which would not have incorporated easily in the attempt we have made to demonstrate the significance of du Maurier's art in general.

Taken in the order in which they are printed here, the first illustrations show the range of effect and variety of line which the artist was afterwards to narrow into the conventions by which he is now chiefly remembered. But if such an effect as that in the picture *Caution*, for instance, would not have been possible with him in his last period, it was because the nature of the subjects required on the journal which absorbed most of his energies afforded no stimulus for anything so Rembrandtesque. He brought such possibilities of style over from his romantic period in *The Cornhill Magazine*, and it must be admitted that the effect in this drawing seems too powerful for the music-hall comedy it has to carry off.

A picture bewitching on account of the grace it contains is that called "Berkeley Square." Du Maurier had quickly perceived that the quality of grace could well survive side by side with any amount of humour. It is interesting to try and imagine what Phil May would have made of the scene. It was intended for a poignant one, but it becomes chiefly a very attractive one in du Maurier's hands, the pathos lying with the wording rather than the picture.

The drawing affords us many characteristics of his work. The lady in white reclining in the vehicle is a very embodiment of elegance, and the discerning drawing that defines the coachman repays observation, as also the "style" with which the white horse is swiftly

111

shaded in. It was once the custom for the carriages of people in fashion to draw up under the trees in Berkeley Square, in summer, for tea brought out from Gunter's. Last summer one of the evening papers asked the question why the custom had lapsed. Du Maurier's drawing of the scene was accompanied by the following lines, which perhaps provide the answer.

SKETCH FOR INITIAL LETTER IN "THE CORNHILL"
OCTOBER, 1883.

BERKELEY SQUARE, 5 P.M.

The weather is warm as I walk in the Square,
And observe her barouche standing tranquilly there,
It is under the trees, it is out of the sun,
In the corner where Gunter retails a plain bun.

How solemn she looks, I have seen a mute merrier—
Plumes a sky-blue, and her pet a sky-terrier—
The scene is majestic, and peaceful, and shady,
Miss Humble sits facing: I pity that lady.

Her footman goes once, and her footman goes twice,
Ay, and each time returning he brings her an ice.
The patient Miss Humble receives, when he comes,
A diminutive bun; let us hope it has plums!

Now is not this vile. When I tickle my chops,
Which I frequently do, I subside into shops:
We do not object to this solemn employment,
But why *afficher* such material enjoyment?

Some beggars stand by—I extremely regret it—
They wish for a taste. Don't they wish they may get it?
She thus aggravates both the humble and needy,
You'll own she is thoughtless, perhaps she is greedy.

The pictures "Queen Prima Donna" and "Proxy" are two early nursery scenes of the many du Maurier contributed to *Punch*. They show the style, the flowing and painter-like stroke of the pen that revealed such a Rossetti-like sense of material beauty in his earlier drawings—a style worthy of the refinement of the subject in "Proxy," the charm in it of sentiment that humour strengthens rather than displaces. The drawing expresses childhood, in circumstances where it can expand without loss of bloom through contention with unhappy circumstances. It shows the human beauty that expands from the conserved force of life when it has not to contend with unfavourable environment. Beauty is perhaps the one certain result of favourable environment. The ideal within "Socialism" which makes even its opponents Socialists is the aspiration that some day everyone will be favourably environed.

§2

It was a long while before the result of always working for a comic paper took effect on du Maurier. Not for some time did the knowledge that everything can be made to appear ridiculous persuade the artist to believe with his editor that everything is ridiculous. The humour of his subjects is still a part and not the whole of those subjects in his art, and this was all to the glory of the great comic paper in which he drew, for the humour of nothing in the world is the whole of that thing. Farce represents it so to be. Du Maurier had no genius for Farce. He responded to actual life; Farce is artificial; it is thus that the beauty and charm as well as the humour of life were involved in his representations.

Humour for humour's sake has brought about the downfall of every comic paper that has tried it. *Punch* has been saved from it by the wilful seriousness of some of its contributors. Every now and then, with something like "The Song of the Shirt" or, in another vein, a cartoon of Tenniel's, *Punch* has been brought back to Reality and thus to the only source of humour.

In the drawing "Honour where Honour is Due" the point is made in the legend, but the illustration illuminates it rather brutally. It is a picture in which we find du Maurier expressing the prejudices of the old régime against the *nouveau riche*. It illustrates a prejudice rather than a fact. It was not at all true in Victoria's reign that money would carry a man anywhere. In that time the man with money only but without birth wanted better manners than the man with everything else but money to get him into Society. It was less the objectionableness of trade—as du Maurier in such a drawing as this tried to imply—than the advance of it that the old aristocracy really resented.

A drawing characteristic of the artist's work in the eighties—in 1880 to be definite—is that entitled "Mutual Admirationists." It really dates itself. It is descriptive of one of the moods of "passionate

Brompton." The satire of the three admiring ladies is perfect. In our own time ladies have gazed like this at genius. Sometimes genius is really there, sometimes it is not—but the profound and undying belief of women in it, often expressed beautifully as well as absurdly, is the rain from heaven enabling it to thrive. In the expressive drawing of the faces and the bearing of the three ladies in this picture we have du Maurier's real humour—its reality in its closeness to life, and his genius in expressing through contour the whole tale of strange æsthetic enthusiasm.

In an earlier part of the book we showed that the artist exposed "æstheticism" from the inside. He hardly draws any figures so happily as those of bored, poetic youths. In *Sic Transit Gloria Mundi* he does not depict "The Duke" of the scene half so convincingly as the young gossip talking to the Duchess. No one else in the world could have drawn so well that young man, with his weak, but Oxford voice—it is almost to be heard—and tired but graceful manners.

The drawing "Post-Prandial Pessimists" is not so sympathetic— which means that it is not so intimate in touch and full of knowledge. The straight mechanical lines with which the clothes are drawn are rather meaningless. This treatment represents a convention, and a bad one, because it covers the paper without really conveying the elasticity of clothing or the animation of muscle determining its folds. At this stage of his career du Maurier has begun to work rather mechanically and by a recipe; he is less curious of form as it actually is to be observed, and more content with just making a drawing in as neat and as businesslike a way as possible, with the wording of the legend uppermost in his thoughts. The artist is disappearing in the "Punch Artist." The drawing of detail, for instance, inclines to be blotty; it is no longer affectionately done. At least the pre-Raphaelite in du Maurier is now dead. The artist's early drawings, where his native tastes break into expression, are pre-Raphaelite in feeling. He made a bad impressionist, a thoroughly bad imitator of Keene's success with impressionism. He lost what was most his own when he "threw over" his belief in glamour, and took to laughing at his own enthusiasms; when he ceased to confine

115

his mockery to things that he hated, as he hated the æsthetic movement. The gods revenged his satire of the inspiration of the pre-Raphaelites in the Tale of Camelot by taking that inspiration away from himself.

"SIC TRANSIT GLORIA MUNDI!"

"BY THE WAY, DUCHESS, SUPPOSING THAT WE DO SUCCEED IN GETTING THE HOUSE OF LORDS ABOLISHED THIS SESSION, WON'T IT BE A GREAT BLOW TO THE DUKE?"

"YES, IF HE EVER HEARS OF IT; BUT I SHAN'T TELL HIM, YOU KNOW!"

PUNCH, MARCH 22, 1884.

The drawing "Things one would rather have expressed Differently" represents du Maurier's final phase at its very best. It has the precision of workmanship of a thing executed to a well-tried recipe. It is dainty as well as precise; and still in the way the dimpling of soft dress fabric is touched in, sympathetic, and characteristic of the earlier du Maurier. It belongs to the *Trilby* period, but is better than the illustrations to *Trilby*.

§ 3

The unpublished sketches which we have been allowed to reproduce from du Maurier's private sketch-book, and which we are using as end pieces, are very interesting. In the strictest artistic sense there is very little of the art of pen-drawing to-day. In the work done with the pen for modern illustration the inking-in is too much of an after process of ink upon pencil work. The quality of the drawing is really determined by the pencil, which is the actual medium of work. In going over the pencil work the ink-line follows it in many cases so closely that it cannot assert the characteristics of penmanship. But in making preliminary small studies for a picture with the pen, an artist, feeling less necessity for a certain kind of accuracy, often uses the pen much more freely, sympathetically, and happily because he is actually drawing with it and not merely following over forms determined first in another medium. We have printed the reproductions from the sketch-book about their original size. Many of them express the freer qualities of real pen-drawing—an autographic character in the line-work akin to that secured in original etching. The pen is an instrument that works best on a small scale, in which it can be manipulated flexibly in the fingers; in this it is like the etching-needle itself. The artist working direct with his pen has before him while he draws the actual effect of his ink on paper, instead of having to imagine it in advance while he works out his subject in pencil. The vignette of the man lying back in his chair near the leaded window has qualities in the shadow of the window that we look to find in vain in du Maurier's professional work. It is a sympathetic pen-drawing; the lines express much more than a formula—they secure a dramatic play of shadow.

This memorandum—for that is what the drawing is—was, we believe, never used by du Maurier, though some of the sketches appearing here—that, for instance, of the lady with a child in her arms, and that of the girl in a window-seat, wearing a frilled dress— can be found serving as initial letters and head-pieces in the early *Cornhill Magazines*, carried no farther in finish than they are here.

So far as one can judge from the study for an illustration to *Wives and Daughters*, which we print with the illustration as it actually appeared in the *Cornhill*, seems to show that the artist could carry the conception of a drawing a long way without reference to a model. The sketch of the girl near the window affords us, in its Whistlerian suggestiveness and refinement, another instance of the purely artistic qualities which some critics have denied du Maurier the ability to secure, his professional ready style being too quickly accepted as completely expressing to the full his artistic nature. Du Maurier seems to have purchased his great journalistic and worldly success at the expense of qualities not altogether dissimilar from those shown in the works of Whistler, his companion at the beginning of his career. The pen sketch referred to of the girl by the window, the soft shadow outlining her face and falling upon the chair, the play of the line that suggests the contour of her figure, all reveal something of the refined skill, economy, and sensitiveness of expression that distinguished everything of Whistler's.

And du Maurier's handwriting—witness the manuscript for his French version of Byron's "Sun of the sleepless—melancholy star!" which appeared in the *Illustrated Magazine*—is characteristic of an exquisite artist in its pleasant nervous beauty of style. It is the writing of one who could have etched. Etching demands only the most autographic features of a man's draughtsmanship; it prevents him from spreading himself in the irrelevancies of space-covering lines necessary in work done to meet the demand of the Editor's measure. The demand must have its effect on those who meet it, in diluting the intimate quality of their work, so that it is not always easy to estimate the real strength of artistic impulse in it.

As art becomes more self-expressive it becomes more subjective; it demands that the student of it shall enter into the artist's feelings; it does not go out to meet him and explain itself after the fashion of the humbler forms of illustration with their purely objective ideal. It is only an educated public that will allow an illustrator the spontaneous style of drawing that some of the wittiest French illustrators indulge in. In England the demand for what is wrongly inferred to be good draughtsmanship has quenched spontaneity in illustration.

Photographs, which are driving pen illustrations out of the illustrated papers, are in themselves many of them highly artistic and beautiful, but in another sense familiarity with photographs has damaged the public sense of art and lost us the taste for merry, irresponsible freedom of drawing. There was no poverty in du Maurier's skill in illustration; but one is compelled to believe his resources as an artist never fully revealed themselves for the lack of the encouragement which only a small cultivated public is prepared to give. He reconciled himself to the big public with its less refined standard. His companion Whistler remained loyal to the few who, by their quick response, could follow the work of his genius in its last refinements. Du Maurier had more artistic energy than Whistler, but he lived in a less exalted artistic mood. Comparison of this kind would be irrelevant but for the fact that behind all du Maurier's work in *Punch* there seems to hover an artist of a different kind from the one which it was possible for Mr. Punch to employ.

POST-PRANDIAL PESSIMISTS

SCENE—THE SMOKING-ROOM AT THE DECADENTS.

FIRST DECADENT (M.A., OXON.). "AFTER ALL, SMYTHE, WHAT WOULD LIFE BE WITHOUT COFFEE?"

SECOND DECADENT (B.A., CAMB.). "TRUE, JEOHNES, TRUE! AND YET, AFTER ALL, WHAT IS LIFE WITH COFFEE?"

PUNCH, OCTOBER 15, 1892.

§4

Sometimes we hear critics discussing whether beauty is or is not the object of Art. As a matter of fact it does not really matter much whether beauty is the object, since it is always the result of true art. Craft is the language of an artist's sympathies—inspiration flagging at the point where sympathy evaporates. The quality of craft is the barometer of the degree of the artist's response to some aspect of life. Absence of beauty in craftsmanship indicates absence of inspiration, the failure to respond to life.

Though du Maurier fell short of Keene in breadth of inspiration, there were still aspects of life which he represented better than that master, phases of life which he approached with greater eagerness. He expressed perfectly once and for all in art the life of the drawing-room in the great days of the drawing-room, as did Watteau the life of the Court in the great days of a Court. Men take their rank in art by expressing completely something which others have expressed incidentally.

There is now the glamour of the past upon du Maurier's work in *Punch*. The farther we are away in distance of time from the date of the execution of a work of art the more legendary and fabulous its tale becomes. In good work forgotten costumes seem bizarre but not preposterous. Whenever in a picture a thing looks preposterous—except in the art of caricature, and du Maurier was not a caricaturist—the representation of it in the picture is a bad one. We never find in the paintings of Vandyke, Velasquez, Gainsborough, or other great artists, however difficult the period of fashion with which they had to deal, anything preposterous—always something beautiful, however unreasonable in ornamentation and clothes. Sometimes it is said that beauty and simplicity are the same. But we have to remember that complexity remains simple whilst unconsciousness of complexity remains. There were several periods of dress that retained beauty and complexity side by side. We find beauty to-day in the avoidance of complexity, because, being at last really civilised, we are impatient of irrelevance even in dress. Du Maurier was never for a moment conscious that there was in all the rigmarole of Victorian costume and decoration anything redundant.

He seemed to take, in decoration for instance, the draped mantelpiece with its bows of ribbons, and pinned fans quite as seriously as Velasquez took the hooped skirt in costume. Artifice is fascinating in those with whom it is natural to be artificial. When du Maurier thought he recognised merely a passing "fashion" and hit out at it, he made far less interesting pictures for posterity than when he took the outward aspect of the age he lived in as being in the natural order of things.

§5

The Victorian age—which invented *Punch*, the greatest humorous paper the world has ever known—had no sense of humour. It was the age of serious people. The secret of the character of *Punch* as an organ of satire is that it represents the times, scorning only what the English people scorn. This representative attitude is, I believe, quite puzzling to many editors of foreign publications, who seem to conceive the business of satire to be mockery of everything.

At one happy period of its career *Punch* set itself a very high artistic standard. The paper intended to avail itself of the services of whatever artistic genius it could attach to itself by attractive emoluments. It then pieced out its satiric business among its distinguished staff, above everything else artists, perhaps not one of them animated with that fervour of attack which is the genius of foreign caricature. These men, by their several temperaments, founded the characteristics and traditions of *Punch*. They were perfectly friendly, not at all anxious to make themselves unpleasant; and the traditions of *Punch* remain the same to this day. It would always rather laugh with people than against them.

§6

Du Maurier's novels are a proof of what an illustrator he was by nature; he seemed to conceive matter and illustration together. It would be strange to read either of his novels without their drawings. Probably his tales would have failed of their immediate success but for the wealth of admirable illustration which make them unique among novels. The illustrations increase perceptibly the appeal of the text. The draughtsmanship is so well identified with its purpose, that we think of it always in connection with a "page." In these days, when art editors think that any picture reduced to size will make an "illustration," it is pleasant to take down our old *Punches*. Qualities of impressionism which are everything in a picture hanging on a wall to be seen across the breakfast table, will seldom be made suitable for book-embellishment simply by process of reduction.

Du Maurier established a more intimate relationship with the public who admired his drawings than any humorous artist has. In America, where for many years the opinion of English Society seems to have been formed from his drawings, the unseen author of them was thought of quite affectionately. The immediate success of his novels there took its rise from this fact. The personal letters which he received from America with the success of *Trilby* ran into many hundreds. There must have been something to account for all this— some curious flavour in everything he did, just one of those secret influences which so often put the technical rules of criticism out of court in dealing with an artist's work.

He succeeded to Leech in the Society subjects, but he himself has not had a successor in these themes. No one has been able to enter the same field as worthily, for instance, as Mr. Raven-Hill entered a field once worked by Keene. There have been better draughtsmen—from the photographic point of view—than du Maurier attempting to fill his place. But "a place" on a newspaper can only be filled by a personality. It is artistic personality that has been wanting in recent years in *Punch* on the side of the fashionable satire which Leech and du Maurier successively had made their own.

We have pointed out that his work in *Punch* was at its best when he was going most into Society. That is characteristic of all artists—that their inspiration flames or dies in proportion to the immediacy of their contact with actuality. Having chosen the world for his theme, he could make nothing of it when he ceased to go out. In his earlier and middle period, living in evening-clothes, he drew with an inexhaustible impulse. When he thought he had his "world" by heart and could reconstruct with the aid of some obliging friends who consented to pose, he gave us pleasant pictures of his friends posing, but the great record he had put together in the sixties, seventies, the early eighties of the London of his time was at an end. Then it was that he repeated his formulæ, his "Things one would have expressed otherwise," and others of like series without introducing any freshness of situation, carrying out the brief dialogues with figures in which there was little variation of character—as little variation as there is in the same model employed on two different days. All this has been touched upon in this book, but we must insist upon it, for the memory of the real du Maurier has nothing so much to fear as our memory of du Maurier when he was, as an artist, not quite himself.

THINGS ONE WOULD RATHER HAVE EXPRESSED
DIFFERENTLY

FAIR HOSTESS. "GOOD-NIGHT, MAJOR JONES. WE'RE SUPPOSED TO BREAKFAST AT NINE; BUT WE'RE NOT VERY PUNCTUAL PEOPLE. INDEED, THE LATER YOU APPEAR TO-MORROW MORNING, THE BETTER PLEASED WE SHALL ALL BE!"

MAY 13, 1893.

We hope we have performed the funeral of the less deserving side of his work, thereby releasing the immortal part of it to the fuller recognition due to it from connoisseurs.

All du Maurier's drawings in his best period are distinguished by the sharpness of contrast between black and white in them. Ruskin, whilst approving in his *Art of England* of du Maurier's use of black to indicate colour, thought he carried the black and white contrast to chess-board pattern excess. In later years, submitting to the influence of Keene's method, in which black is always used to secure effects of tone instead of colour, du Maurier's style underwent a transformation which, from the purely artistic point of view, was not to its advantage. Keene's method was justified in his extreme sensitiveness to what painters define as "values"—the relation in tone of one surface to another. This particular kind of sensitiveness was not characteristic of du Maurier's vision, nor was a style so dependent upon subtlety of the kind suited to express his mind. And here it is interesting to emphasise the connection which is so often overlooked between temperament and style. In the observation of human character itself du Maurier always perceived the broad and distinctive features; the broad ones of type rather than the subtle ones of individuals; things for him were either black or white, beautiful or ugly. The twilight in which beauty and ugliness merge, in which the heroic and the villainous mingle, was unknown to him—a region in which the white figure of a hero is as impossible as the black one of a real villain. He observes subtly enough the airs of those who interest him, but he is not interested in everybody. He doesn't think much of people who, through lack either of physical or moral stature, can enter the drawing-room unperceived. He is not sympathetic to neutral characters. It was because the Victorians cultivated magnificence that his somewhat rhetorical art described them with such reality. His pictures were a mirror to the age. Keene was like Shakespeare—the types he drew might change in costume with the times, but would reappear in every generation. But du Maurier only drew Victorians. And thus his art has that vivid local colour which is the vital characteristic of effective satire.

It is significant that the artist had nursed throughout his youth an enthusiasm for Byron. Until the influence of Mr. Bernard Shaw had chilled the air, England remained under the spell of that romantic poet. The Victorians in everything betrayed the love of glamour. They exalted the unknown Disraeli out of sheer delight at his Byronic ability to irradiate everything with romance. There has

never been a moment like the present in which there is a complete absence of pride in tradition, which is pleasure in romance. But the reason is simple. Our traditions belong to the pre-Industrial time. The romance of the Victorians was a last glow in the sky. We might even go as far as to read an occult significance into the art of Turner, the great painter of the sunset. We nowadays go back to du Maurier's pictures, where the after-glow remains, and they seem separated from us by something thicker than time, as if a great wall had been built up between the age of the twopenny tube and that of the carriage-and-pair. And lest there should remain a link between them, over which we might be sentimental, the face of Buckingham Palace is to be despoiled, the long grey outline, characteristic of English monarchy in its reticence and repose, is, we imagine, to give place to something in the image of a prosperous Insurance Office.

Already du Maurier's art is very precious; the environment of the people whom he depicted is everywhere being smashed up. Our curiosity is sharpened for everything that remains to reflect those people to us. Our debt to the mirror of du Maurier's art increases every hour.

CPSIA information can be obtained at www.ICGtesting.com
Printed in the USA
LVOW12s0224090415

433871LV00001B/90/P